LONDON'S
100
STRANGEST
PLACES

LONDON'S
100
STRANGEST
PLACES

DAVID LONG

The
History
Press

First published 2018

The History Press
The Mill, Brimscombe Port
Stroud, Gloucestershire, GL5 2QG
www.thehistorypress.co.uk

British Library Cataloguing in Publication Data.
A catalogue record for this book is available from the British Library.

ISBN 978 0 7509 8763 9

Typesetting and origination by The History Press
Printed and bound in Great Britain by TJ International Ltd

CONTENTS

INTRODUCTION

London. It is not a pleasant place; it is not agreeable, or cheerful, or easy … it is only magnificent.

Henry James (1843–1916)

Dr Johnson advised his companion Boswell, 'Sir, if you wish to have a just notion of the magnitude of this city, you must not be satisfied with seeing its great streets and squares, but must survey its innumerable little lanes and courts' – and more than two centuries later his advice is equally valid.

A vibrant, living organism encompassing more than 600 square miles and twenty centuries of human experience and endeavour, London may be home to millions, be visited every year by millions more and be as well documented as any great world city, yet – almost 2,000 years after Rome's elderly military commander Aulus Plautius first bridged the Thames near Billingsgate – it still keeps its secrets.

Now, this companion volume to *London's 100 Most Extraordinary Buildings* lifts the lid on a few of the best, revealing some of the capital's most curious corners and the history behind them.

From ancient courtyards often hidden from view to the tangle of tunnels which run beneath the streets, it tells the strange stories of some genuine oddities: a street lamp powered by sewer gas; the one street in London where you can legally drive on the wrong side of the road; a Russian tsar working incognito in a vanished naval dockyard; even a Nazi memorial sited among the heroes and adventurers of the British Empire.

Written as much for the inquisitive armchair traveller as for the well-informed London resident, for the first-time traveller or regular visitor, the fact that most of these places are accessible to the public – and often at no charge – means this book provides the best possible start for anyone who wishes to get off the beaten track and under the skin of the hidden city that is modern-day London.

David Long
www.davidlong.info

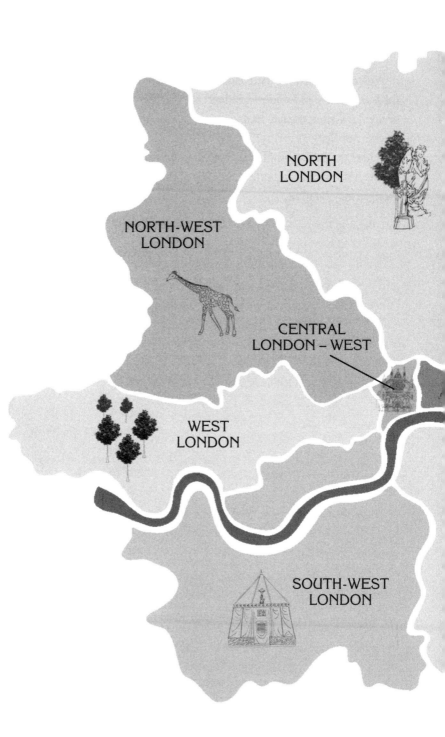

NORTH
LONDON

NORTH-WEST
LONDON

CENTRAL
LONDON – WEST

WEST
LONDON

SOUTH-WEST
LONDON

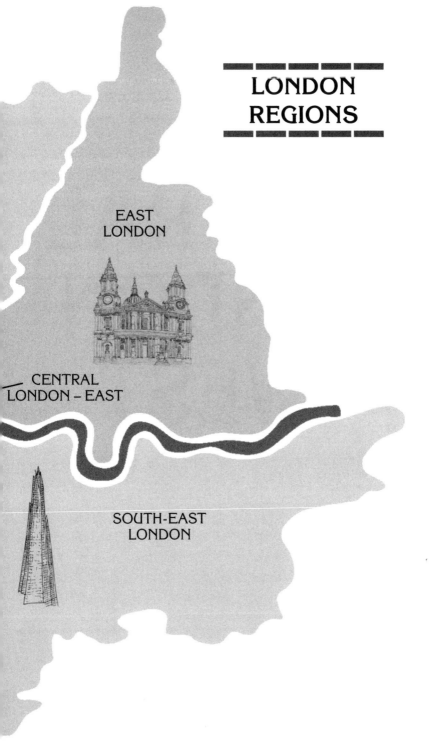

LONDON
REGIONS

EAST
LONDON

CENTRAL
LONDON – EAST

SOUTH-EAST
LONDON

CENTRAL LONDON -WEST

CORAM'S FIELDS
GUILFORD STREET, WC1

No Unaccompanied Adults

Calling itself 'seven acres of freedom', this central London park and playground is unusual in that adults are allowed in only if accompanied by a child. But then perhaps that's only as it should be, since the park we see today occupies a small part of the 56-acre site acquired by a wealthy seafarer for another famously child-focused enterprise, the Foundling Hospital. There is a relic of the hospital in this pillar by the entrance, a structure which once held a revolving niche containing what old Captain Thomas Coram called his All-Comers Basket. Using this, mothers keen to avoid legal entanglement or moral censure could simply deposit their unwanted infants anonymously, rather than leaving them 'to die on dunghills' as the good Captain put it.

It was an inspired idea, but proved too successful for its own good and on the first day of its operation in 1742 a staggering 117 babies were left in precisely this manner. In the next few weeks, another 425 arrived and before long this chaotic (if well-meaning) admissions policy had to be abandoned. Instead, a balloting scheme was introduced to decide who gained entry: a white ball admitted the child once he or she had passed a medical examination; a red ball secured a place on the waiting list; a black ball indicated rejection, meaning alternative arrangements would have to be found elsewhere.

Demand for places continued to outstrip spaces, however, so that new rules were instituted allowing, for example, only one baby per unmarried mother to be admitted, and then only when the child was under 12 months old, had been deserted by its father, and where the mother had been of good character before her 'fall'.

The expense of running such an establishment was naturally considerable, but the Foundling Hospital was fortunate in that it enjoyed the patronage of a number of high-profile supporters. These included not just Coram's original committee of twenty-one ladies 'of Nobility and Distinction' who petitioned the King for support, but also the artist Hogarth – who became a governor and with other artists contributed a number of valuable portraits – and G.F. Handel who presented an organ to the hospital chapel and raised an incredible £7,000 through his own performances here of his *Messiah*.

Eventually the hospital went, however, moving to Berkhamsted in 1926 when the valuable site was sold for development. Happily, a new band of benefactors (led by the newspaper proprietor Viscount Rothermere) was able to rescue a small portion of it, and when Theodore Jacobsen's hospital buildings were cleared away what remained was laid out to give local children somewhere to play. A place, should they so choose, where they could treat their parents to green and grassy pleasures.

NEW RIVER COMPANY
MYDDLETON SQUARE, WC1

London's Own Aqueduct

Problems with water supply are nothing new. In Elizabeth I's time, the Thames and its tributaries were already badly polluted, the City still had no sewerage system separate from its water supply, and London generally was evil smelling and clearly very unhealthy.

People were nevertheless still getting their water from open water courses. Some depended on water-bearers to bring what they needed in barrels from the various rivers, while others – generally the richer ones – obtained water from shallow wells which tapped ground water supplies or through primitive pipes known as quills. Even these sources were soon contaminated, however, and in 1606 and 1607 two Acts of Parliament were passed permitting the Commonality of the City of London to run a channel to bring fresh water in from two clean Hertfordshire springs.

The task fell to Hugh Myddleton, a goldsmith and well-heeled entrepreneur, who, despite fierce opposition from those landowners across whose estates the channel would pass, agreed to complete the job in just four years. In fact, he struggled until James I agreed to help out financially – Myddleton was well connected and had dealings with the King as a goldsmith – in return for half the profits.

Four years later water flowed from the villages of Great Amwell and Chadwell into the Round Pond by Sadler's Wells, arriving via an open channel 10ft wide, 4ft deep and just under 40 miles long.

Before long the New River Company had four such reservoirs, each 10ft deep and up to 2 acres in area, with water being piped into the City through wooden pipes. Then as now up to 25 per cent was lost owing to pipe bursts and other leakages, but Myddleton was rewarded for his efforts with a baronetcy.

Unfortunately, the public showed less regard for his work and before long, as noted in a hastily commissioned monograph entitled *A Microscopic Examination of the Water Supplies for the Inhabitants of London*, the problems of having an open channel were made obvious. The people of London, it said, 'use it as a resort for bathing in summer and at all times as a receptacle for refuse, animal and vegetable matter'. In short, it was soon as toxic and as disgusting as the Thames water it was meant to replace.

The solution was to import filter beds and filtration works, these being installed at Hornsey and Stoke Newington, which eventually became the London termini of the New River. Closer to town the magnificent headquarters can still be seen on Roseberry Avenue, complete with the lavishly panelled seventeenth-century Oak Room which has been reconstructed within the later building (now apartments). In Claremont Square, there is also one surviving reservoir, railed off and looking for all the world like a prehistoric tumulus.

The course the original river took can still be discerned, however, much of it now landscaped as the New River Walk and turned into public parkland. There is also the evidence of the New River Estate, most of which was sold to Islington Council in the mid 1970s; Colebrook Row and Duncan Terrace, for example, would originally have faced each other across that first channel excavated by Sir Hugh.

ADELPHI
STRAND, WC2

Lottery-Funded Loser

Having grown organically over the centuries (which is to say haphazardly), as a rule elaborate, large-scale planning schemes do not fare well in London – and the fate of the Adam brothers' imposing riverside Adelphi is no exception.

Concerned that their work had hitherto been on too small a scale, or limited to less prestigious commissions outside London, John, Robert, James and William Adam took a ninety-nine-year lease on a substantial plot of land between the river and the Strand in 1768. Paying the Duke of St Albans £1,200 per annum for it, they set about building a quay and several storeys of warehousing in extensive vaults set back from the river.

Relying on cheap labour from their native Scotland – pipers were brought in to keep the workers happy – they planned a series of streets above; two parallel to the river, two running perpendicular to it, with the centrepiece a royal terrace of eleven four-storey stucco and plastered houses overlooking the Thames.

They quickly ran into difficulties, however. Initially, the Corporation of London blocked the development, claiming all rights over the river bed. Then distance from the fashionable West End proved an issue when it came to attracting the right class of tenant (this despite the high-quality interiors by Angelica Kaufmann and G.B. Cipriani). Finally, they suffered a funding shortfall, when the government declined to rent the massive vaults for storing gunpowder for fear of flooding at high tide.

Fortunately, the brothers were not without influence and a special Act of Parliament in 1773 allowed them to rescue the scheme by holding a lottery. The following year 4,370 tickets were offered at Jonathan's Coffee House on Cornhill, at a hefty £50 a throw.

Certainly, once completed, the forty-one-bay development was (if only briefly) highly impressive when viewed from the river, with an attractive centre and the façade closed by the projecting terraces in Robert and Adam Street. Admittedly the crisp neo-Classicism and decorated pilasters of the eleven houses did not appeal to the architectural establishment, but the artistic elite liked what it saw immensely and David Garrick, Thomas Hood, John Galsworthy and others subsequently moved in.

By 1870, though, the construction of the Victoria Embankment had cut off the warehouses from the river. These quickly fell into disuse, providing what a contemporary chronicler called a dismal haunt for street thieves, a place where 'the most abandoned characters pass the night, nestling on foul straw'. Two years later the terrace was cemented over and had its ironwork removed, before eventually it was torn down and replaced by the block we see today. Somewhat inappropriately, this too is called the Adelphi, meaning, of course, 'brothers'.

Today, sadly, just small fragments of the original remain, including 7 Adam Street, 1–3 Robert Street and 4–6 John Street, alongside the pretty Royal Society of Arts. Some of the vaulting can also be seen from Lower Robert Street, but it is still hard to get a fair impression of the very considerable scope and scale of the brothers' short-lived achievement.

ASTOR HOUSE
TEMPLE PLACE, WC2

Faked, but with Finesse

Originally the London estate office of William Waldorf Astor – the first Viscount Astor was nicknamed 'Walled-Orf' after taking the necessary steps to prevent members of the public strolling through his Cliveden estate – 2 Temple Place these days provides a welcome relief from the brutal presence of the monolithic Howard Hotel nearby.

For Astor, the 1895 building formed an important part of his English Plan, a bid to revert to his European roots after recognising that while his native America was a fine place to do business, 'why travelled people of independent means should remain there more than a week is not readily to be comprehended'.

To this end, created for one duke, let to another, rebuilt by a third and inherited by a fourth (respectively Buckingham, Gloucester, Sutherland and Westminster), Cliveden was just the ticket. Perfect for an American as hell-bent as Astor on acquiring the titles and trappings of an English toff, it had been designed by Sir Charles Barry and built high above the loveliest stretch of the Thames on the very spot where 'Rule, Britannia' was first performed.

Crucially, it was also for sale: the Duke of Westminster already having a seat when he was given Cliveden by his mother-in-law – but being badly in need of money. Astor, of course, had plenty of this – an estimated $175 million from his father – but needed a seat. Accordingly, £250,000 changed hands, giving

Westminster the liquidity he required and Astor the great house and its contents. (Later the Duke realised he had left some valuable paintings behind, which Astor promptly returned, though he retained a 200-year-old visitors' book which he insisted went with the house.)

Other acquisitions rapidly followed as Waldorf and then his son cemented their foundations in London and English society. These included 18 Carlton House Terrace, Hever Castle in Kent, a fleet of horse-drawn carriages controversially painted in the same chocolate-brown livery favoured by the royal family, the *Observer* newspaper and the influential *Pall Mall Gazette*. Also, in time, another grand ducal establishment in St James's Square – now home to the Naval & Military Club, but originally built for the first Duke of Kent – and the 55-carat 'Sanci' diamond which at various times had been the property of Charles the Bold, Charles I's queen, Henrietta Maria, and Louis XIV.

Together with his extensive US holdings, it was a considerable real-estate and business empire, all of which the Astors controlled from this small but robust Portland stone castle with its charming early Elizabethan styling.

Designed by John Loughborough Pearson, its Great Hall and Library were located on the first floor to take advantage of the river views. Astor's money meant the elaborate detailing continued inside too, with an ornate gallery of ebony columns and silver-gilt panelling, carvings of many literary figures and lavish glazing with ornate stained glass. Finally, and in recognition of a family which had crossed the Atlantic in such triumph, the gilded, beaten-copper weathervane above the roof includes a representation of the *Santa Maria*, the caravel which carried Christopher Columbus on his pioneering voyage across the same great ocean.

GOODWIN'S COURT
ST MARTIN'S LANE, WC2

Predating Savile Row

It is tempting to think that, in the summer of 1763, Samuel Johnson must have had in mind humble little backwaters like this one when he encouraged his companion Boswell, newly arrived in London, to 'survey its innumerable little lanes and courts'.

These days very much an accidental discovery for the strolling visitor to Covent Garden, the buildings of Goodwin's Court are charming rather than architecturally important, intimate rather than impressive. Nevertheless, the short walk from one end to the other gives one a fine impression of another Covent Garden, one far less grand or planned than the Earl of Bedford's nearby piazza, which was a truly radical innovation for London in its day.

By comparison, to most visitors, Goodwin's Court must seem positively Dickensian. Although that said, with its blackened timbers, worn steps, comically bulging windows and bowed walls, it actually predates Dickens (even his earliest writings) by well over 130 years. In fact, it makes its first appearance in the rate books in 1690, being described then as a row of tailors.

Having on its south side an intact row of eight narrow, yet desirable, late eighteenth-century shopfronts with two floors of living accommodation provided above, it is certainly wider and considerably more salubrious than nearby, quite nasty Brydges Place (which at its narrowest is barely more than a foot and a half wide). It is nevertheless still rather more of an alleyway than a court, and, as such, is a highly unusual survivor in an area such as Covent Garden, which has seen more than its fair share ot reshaping and redevelopment since the Earl's man, Inigo Jones, was first at work here in the 1630s.

Inevitably much of its charm depends on it being so easy to miss: the entrance from St Martin's Lane being no more than a doorway off the street with a couple of steps down. As a result, most people simply never stumble upon it, but for those who do it is worth studying in detail.

With working gas lamps outside No. 1 and the attractive clock face over the archway giving on to Bedfordbury, it makes a fine contrast with its self-consciously much grander surroundings. Notice too, the metal plates or 'fire-marks' affixed to the buildings, dating from a time before the various privately paid-for groups of watermen and firefighters amalgamated to form the London Fire Engine Establishment. Until this was reformed into the publicly funded London Fire Brigade we know today, at the height of a blaze these plates would have indicated which buildings were insured against fire, thereby encouraging the firemen to concentrate on saving them rather than any adjacent, uninsured properties. It presumably worked, hence Goodwin Court's happy survival into the twenty-first century.

HOLBORN–KINGSWAY SUBWAY
LANCASTER PLACE, WC2

A Tunnel for Trams

It would be nice to think that the last of London's 2,500 tramcars might have been accorded the honour of a plinth in the Science Museum. But, in fact, the vehicle in question (E/3-1904) is known to have met a rather more ignominious end after being deliberately rolled over in July 1952 and set alight on an anonymous siding in Charlton.

Such was the sad, low-key end for this enduring mode of transport, one which had carried up to seven million passengers a year before being deemed to have reached the end of the line. Particularly so when one considers that, after being introduced to London almost 100 years earlier by the aptly named George Train, trams had proved sufficiently popular that, when E/3-1904 made her final run from Westminster to Woolwich, many thousands turned out to see her, some even placing pennies on to the tramlines to obtain a small, bent souvenir of the occasion.

Happily, though, while the trams themselves may be gone, and many hundreds of miles of lines pulled up, covered over or converted for telecommunications lines, some traces of the old network still remain.

By far the largest of these is the Holborn–Kingsway Subway of 1908. For the last thirty years, with the addition of a new approach from Waterloo Bridge, it has been used as a traffic underpass linking Waterloo to Holborn. But originally it was a tram tunnel, simple cut-and-cover for most of its length, but deep level where it crossed the Strand. Running along the length of Kingsway as far as Theobald's Road, it would then have had a flag-waving guard to warn drivers as the trams emerged into daylight on their way to New Cross Gate, Woolwich and Abbey Wood.

By the early 1930s, however, the arched roof had already been replaced by higher steel sections thereby allowing the tunnel to be used by newfangled double-deckers, and it was clear the writing was already on the wall for the trams. At one point, expensive plans were advanced to run them underground – from Bayswater to Aldgate, and from the Holloway Road to the Elephant and Castle – but these were shelved as the more modern and efficient Tube already fulfilled just such a function.

As a result, in London at least, trams quickly passed into history. A year after the destruction of car E/3-1904, the subway was redeployed to store 120 retired buses in case they were needed for the Coronation, and two years after that it served as a railway tunnel in the film *Bhowani Junction*. A film company then offered to take over the subway to use as a studio, but this was disallowed owing to the fire risk and the subway was closed.

Even so its route can still be traced today simply by following the ironwork running down the centre of Southampton Row. These grilles also guard the entrance to another of the tunnel's more recent occupants, namely the Greater London Council's flood control centre, which somewhat paradoxically was sited underground and right above a major sewer. Close by, the old Theobald's Road tram station is apparently still intact and undisturbed, but is unfortunately not open to visitors.

LINCOLN'S INN
CHANCERY LANE, WC2

Peaceful Now, but a Grisly Past

With fourteenth-century origins, buildings dating back to 1489, and Cromwell, Donne, Thomas More and at least seven prime ministers among its alumni, Lincoln's Inn may not share Inner and Middle Temples' romantic Crusader roots, but it remains a fascinating piece of secret, legal London and a delightful place in which to wander.

The name is mysterious, being derived from either the third Earl of Lincoln or Thomas de Lyncoln. Certainly, it is the former's crest, a *lion rampant purpure*, which appears on the early sixteenth-century gatehouse. On the other hand, Lyncoln was the King's Serjeant of Holborn, so he too may have a claim.

What is known is that the Honourable Society of Lincoln's Inn has been on its present site only since 1422, although it was clearly active elsewhere before 1348. When it moved here, it was to a house owned by the bishops of Chichester, a fact commemorated by local street names such as Chichester Rents and Chancery (or Chancellor) Lane after one of their number, who became Chancellor of England. In 1580, however, the Society purchased the freehold of this property (for £520) so that today one can stroll from the riverside to Camden – that is from Inner Temple to the Law Courts, then through this place to Gray's Inn – almost without placing a foot outside one or other of the capital's historic legal enclaves.

Here, as one enters through the red and blue brick gatehouse of 1518, the parallels with an Oxbridge college are obvious. A rich and diverse collection of picturesque buildings, many of them sixteenth- and seventeenth-century houses more recently converted to office use, these are arranged around four loosely connected squares, two of which are nicely enclosed (Old Square and Old Buildings) while New Square and the space before the chapel are more open.

Unusually the latter's undercroft is open too, for the last 400 years providing somewhere for students and lawyers 'to walk and talk and confer for their learnings'. The library is also notable, rebuilt by the Hardwicks in 1843 but founded in 1497, making it London's oldest such institution.

Immediately to the west, Lincoln's Inn Fields, with its 12 acres of lawns and plane trees, is London's largest square; to one side a plaque commemorates former resident Spencer Perceval (1762–1812), now remembered merely as the only prime minister to have been assassinated. Shot in the Commons by an irate Liverpudlian, his murder was foreseen in a dream nine days earlier by John Williams of Redruth, who was dissuaded from journeying to London to warn the authorities.

Despite the proximity of busy High Holborn and Kingsway, the Fields today are quiet and it is hard to believe this is where, in 1586, many thousands gathered to witness the hanging, drawing and quartering of fourteen Catholic traitors found guilty of plotting to replace Elizabeth with Mary. Also hard to credit is that, in the 1930s, the LCC ordered the lovely gardens to be dug up, excavating 1,430 yards of deep trenches, tunnels and heavily armoured bunkers before lining them with concrete against poisoned-gas attack. What purpose they serve now is unclear, but they are known to survive, although the entrances have been sealed off.

OF ALLEY
YORK PLACE, WC2

Remember My Name

Occupying part of the 7-acre site of one of the great, vanished Strand palaces, York Place commemorates York House which once stood here with its principal façade overlooking extensive gardens running down to the river.

Certainly completed before 1237, this had originally been owned by the bishops of Norwich until the Dissolution in 1536 when Henry VIII conveyed it to Charles Brandon, Duke of Suffolk. Passing via Mary I to the Archbishop of York, it later became the official residence of the Lord Keeper of the Great Seal, before finally coming into the possession of George Villiers, Duke of Buckingham, in 1624.

A favourite of James I, Villiers restored the bishops' old estate which at that time encompassed an incredible fifty houses, ten cottages, four stableblocks and seven interconnecting gardens. He also built the magnificent watergate which still survives, marooned and melancholy in Embankment Gardens. But despite having lavished a fortune on these works – in October 1626 the French ambassador described the results as 'the most richly fitted up than any other I saw' – he preferred to live in Whitehall at Wallingford House and used this ancient but grand riverside mansion merely as a place to entertain his guests.

Following his murder in 1628, however, the Duke's wife removed here but then lost the property during the Civil War. Eventually it was recovered by her son, the second Duke, who married the new owner's daughter before the Restoration. He too used it only for ceremonial purposes and in 1672, with speculators eyeing the potentially valuable site and his Grace finding himself to be extremely heavily mortgaged, he gave permission for the old house to be torn down and the land developed.

At the time it was not uncommon for landlords to have whole streets and squares named after them, and indeed the practice continues today most obviously in the way the fragile egos of time-serving councillors are shored up using just such a method.

Not for the first time, however, Buckingham went a step further. As well as securing £30,000 for the house and gardens, he insisted that the new network of streets and lanes being planned on the site by developer Nicholas Barbon record literally every sound and syllable of his name and title. Thus today we have Buckingham Street, Villiers Street, Duke Street – now part of John Adam Street – and George Street, which was eventually to became York Buildings. Also for a while there was Of Alley, until this too was renamed by somebody clearly lacking a sense of history, and (dare one say it) of humour.

SAVOY COURT
STRAND, WC2

Where it's Right to be Wrong

Built on a steep slope of riverbank land granted by Henry III to the future Count of Savoy – the annual rent in 1246 was three barbed arrows – Savoy Court is the only public road in London on which motorists are obliged to drive on the wrong side of the road.

It's tempting to imagine that this is because for a few short years after Count Peter bequeathed it to the monastery of St Bernard in Montjoux, the land on which the road was built was in a sense French territory. But in reality the monastery held it only very briefly as, in 1270, Queen Eleanor paid 300 marks to get it back in order that she could present it to her second son, Edmund, Earl of Lancaster.

Taking a keen interest in royal lands, his brother Edward I was the first English king to commission a national land survey and to map his country. Thereafter, having assessed the precise extent of his domain, he granted Edmund permission to 'strengthen and fortify' his mansion on this site, a process continued by his son, Henry, Duke of Lancaster, who spent a mammoth £35,000 between 1345 and 1370, creating a house said at the time to be without equal in England.

Today, although part of the Duchy of Lancaster (see p. 226) and therefore still a personal possession of the reigning monarch, the land on which this princely edifice once stood is now occupied by a variety of large but indifferent office developments whose rents continue to flow into the Privy Purse.

Count Peter has not been forgotten entirely, however. Indeed, it is his likeness in bronze and gilt that stands guard over the grand Strand entrance to the hotel which bears his name. Shield in hand and lance held high, from his lofty perch gazing down on Savoy Court, he too might like to imagine that the cars arriving and departing on the right side of the road do so in his honour. But, sadly, the truth is rather more prosaic and has more to do with the tight angle required to turn in from the Strand than any act of homage to the area's erstwhile French owner.

SEWER-POWERED GAS LAMP
CARTING LANE, WC2

Progress in Power in One Small Street

Relying on a genuinely sustainable source of power at least a century before that now familiar phrase became current, the

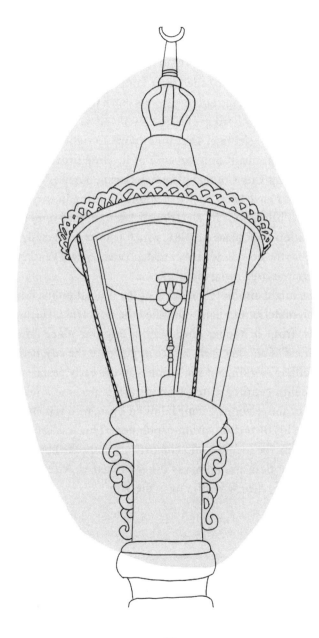

29

delightful-sounding Patent Sewer Ventilating Lantern, which can still be seen in this narrow street running south of the Strand, is sadly the last of its kind remaining.

That at least one of the street lamps in London to draw methane gas from the London sewers down beneath Sir Joseph Bazalgette's embankment has survived is nevertheless something to celebrate. That it has done so right here is also somewhat ironic, if only because of its close proximity to a Westminster City Council plaque declaring the nearby Savoy Theatre to have been 'the first public building in the world to be lit throughout by electricity'. After all, that important innovation took place in 1881, which is to say at exactly the time that the now-suddenly-outdated Patent Sewer Ventilating Lantern was itself being installed.

One might also note the name of the nearest public house, a semi-subterranean hang out called the Coal Hole. The name comes from it having once been a popular place among providers of another early source of power to the city, namely the colliers working on the Thames in the early years of the nineteenth century. Later, by contrast, it became a regular haunt of the celebrated actor Edmund Kean, who was allowed to form his own club-within-a-pub here. This was called the Wolf Club, the membership comprising henpecked husbands who (doubtless among many other things) were reportedly forbidden by their wives to sing in the bath.

SIR JOHN SOANE MUSEUM
LINCOLN'S INN FIELDS, WC2

Home to the Imagination

Since the death of its creator in 1837, one of this country's strangest, most unexpected, most delightful, yet least-known museums, the maze-like home of the most creative architect of his generation seems rarely to get crowded, yet is stuffed full of so many good things.

More than anything it is the perfect memorial for a brilliant man – which is as well since the sad fate of Sir John Soane (1753–1837) has been to see so many of his other buildings destroyed or damaged beyond recognition by later, less skilled hands. Luckily his collection and home have remained intact, both of them painstakingly assembled with the financial help of a rich wife and then preserved by special Act of Parliament which in his lifetime established the place as a public museum.

A prolific and delightfully eccentric collector, Sir John created some fascinating illusions by moving walls and floors, linking spaces through a sequence of highly original rooms, and establishing unusual vertical connections with sunlight flooding in through apertures in the roof. His brilliant use of space, proportion and the manipulation of light in fact set a template which many leading contemporary architects still find inspirational when visiting his home today.

Once this part of his master plan had been accomplished, Soane then set to with the second component, namely filling almost every tiny space between floor and wall with everything interesting he could lay his hands on. From the 3,000-year-old Egyptian sarcophagus of Seti I to a pair of Napoleon's pistols, from rare books to Wren's watch, together with more than 20,000 architectural drawings by himself, Wren again, James and Robert Adam, and many others. There are sculptures too, along with literally hundreds of richly detailed architectural fragments, and paintings by Piranesi, Hogarth – including all eight pictures which comprise *The Rake's Progress* – Canaletto, Reynolds and Turner.

Authentically labyrinthine and free to enter, the resulting treasure trove is the perfect cornucopia of the unusual and unexpected – a sheer delight, in other words, and quite unlike anything else London has to offer. Ordered in a chaotic yet wonderfully romantic fashion (precisely as Soane wished), it has a strong flavour of its creator's favourite ancient Greek and Roman preoccupations and, as one descends into the bowels of the building, an almost monastic or Gothic sense of brooding over the strange and exotic.

Sir John's museum is, in short, unmissable, and not just for the interior either – for, while his designs for Nos 12 and 14 look pretty conventional, finished in brick and Portland stone, Soane applied to the central portion of his triumphant trio the full force of his genius. As a result, with its utterly distinctive façade, projecting first-floor loggia, Coade stone caryatids copied from the Erechtheion at Athens and genuine Gothic pedestals placed between the arched windows (after being removed from niches in the fourteenth-century north front of Westminster Abbey), there is – quite frankly – nothing in the capital to touch it.

SOMERSET HOUSE
STRAND, WC2

The Taxman Taketh

Lost for years to the Inland Revenue, which squandered one of the capital's most dramatic open spaces by using it as a car park, Somerset House has at last been returned to the public and reborn as an arts and exhibition centre with superb views up and down the river.

In fact, the building we see today stands on the site of what had been England's first Renaissance palace. Built in part using stone salvaged from the demolition of the cloisters of the pre-Fire St Paul's, but later much decayed, this was finally demolished in 1775. Its replacement is primarily the work of Sir William Chambers, Comptroller of the Office of Works, who in the name of greater efficiency sought to accommodate in one unified structure various government offices, the Navy Board and three learned bodies: the Royal Academy of Arts, the Royal Society and the Society of Antiquaries.

Initially there was a debate about whether to favour splendour or economy, convenience rather than ornament; but eventually Parliament instructed its architect to produce 'an ornament to the Metropolis and a monument of the taste and elegance of His Majesty's Reign'.

With the King's Bargemaster also to be accommodated, the design had to incorporate access to the Thames, thereby enabling officers of the Navy to travel easily to Deptford and Greenwich. Living quarters had to be provided as well, not just for the Chiefs of Staff but for their cooks, housekeepers, secretaries and so on.

The solution proposed by Chambers was to create, in effect, a series of townhouses arranged around a quadrangle and extending over more than 6 acres. Each government or learned body would be granted a vertical slice of six storeys, although sadly Sir William died before its completion, leaving James Wyatt to carry on and finish the job in 1801.

To maintain the correct scale, two floors of each townhouse were below ground prompting one critic to lament the fate of 'the clerks of the nation [who] in these damp, black and comfortless recesses ... grope about like moles, immersed in Tartarean gloom, where they stamp, sign, examine, indite, doze, and swear'. Others felt the building ('a frightful thing') effectively 'exposed to general derision the bad taste of the King, the Government, and the country'.

But today, perhaps mindful of the problems faced by Chambers – the steeply sloping site, highly unstable ground and the need to make the most of the river frontage – one is inclined to be kinder. Also because increasing congestion – in terms of both traffic and sewage – necessitated the building of the Victoria Embankment, thereby destroying Sir William's carefully considered elevations and removing the building from its river.

Worse was to come, however: mezzanine storeys were introduced to many of the government offices to increase their floor area; and in the 1970s much of the original joinery was removed to meet new fire regulations. Even so, the building still proved inadequate for the bean-counters and, scandalously, much of it was then left empty for nearly two decades.

Eventually common sense prevailed and today, following an extensive programme of restoration, the building, its river terrace and that fabulous central courtyard have been returned to use; together they now comprise one of the most majestic and imaginative cultural venues anywhere in the UK.

WIG & PEN CLUB
STRAND, WC2

A Fragment of Old London

Where Fleet Street runs into the Strand, and where the cities of London and Westminster collide, what was once home to a famous, if undistinguished, club for journalists and lawyers is a unique and extraordinary building.

Usefully located directly opposite the gleaming bulk of the Royal Courts of Justice, the Wig & Pen was tangible evidence of the longstanding ties binding the Fourth Estate and the profession of the Law. But in fact, its origins were far from ancient, as the two separate cliques began congregating here only in 1908.

Despite its messy exterior, the building itself was always more significant, one half being by far the oldest building in the Strand – actually the only one to predate the Great Fire – and for a time home to the Temple gatekeeper. No. 229 indeed dates from as early as 1625 and, with its overhanging first and second floors, is even said to stand on Roman foundations, although the evidence for this is not clear.

Its companion next door was completed in the early eighteenth century, but it is similarly picturesque with its unusual canted bay window. Together they provide the strongest possible contrast, both in style and scale, to the 8-acre Victorian Gothic complex opposite.

Indeed, looking at the older buildings, the two of them squeezed on to the tiniest of sites, it is easy to imagine why the construction of the Law Courts in 1866–68 required the destruction of no fewer than thirty-three separate streets, courtyards and alleyways, the demolition of more than 340 dwellings and sixty commercial buildings, and the eviction of an incredible 4,125 inhabitants. After all, if these two are typical of what stood hereabouts before, the area now covered by the Courts before that date would have been similarly compressed and congested, and above all so completely *medieval.*

As for what replaced it, it was by any standards a massive enterprise: twenty-four courtyards, more than 1,000 rooms all told, and an estimated 35 million bricks concealed behind the gleaming white stone. Also, of course, an epic exercise in urban planning quite beyond the conception of the builders of the two houses pictured here. Dating from an era when London simply grew organically to meet demand – with masons and carpenters building whatever they could cram on to any available plot as the cities of London and Westminster slowly but inexorably blended into one – their time and style had come and gone.

CENTRAL LONDON –EAST

ARMOURY HOUSE
CITY ROAD, EC1

Gentlemen of the Artillery Garden

Like a miniature fortress on the northern border of the City, the headquarters of the Honourable Artillery Company has since 1642 been home to what, if not the oldest regiment in the British Army, is nevertheless the oldest military body in the realm.

Formally established to provide officers for the City's Trained Bands – formed under Henry VIII as the elite militia of the Tudor period – the HAC can actually trace its origins to the reign of Edward III, even if it had to wait until 1537 to be granted a royal charter. That was the year the King addressed a body of archers called the Guild of St George, charging them 'to be overseers of the science of artillerie, that is to witt, long bowes, cross bowes and hand gonnes'.

In fact, Fat Hal is known to have been largely indifferent to mere 'hand gonnes', although he took a great interest in more substantial pieces of weaponry. Thus the principal role of his so-called 'Gentlemen of the Artillery Garden' was to be the defence of the capital – its role 250 years later in restoring order to the City of London following the Gordon Riots was rewarded with a gift of cannon from the City Corporation – although from the start, various members served overseas as well, for example with the fleet against the Armada.

Then, as now, it was nevertheless only a volunteer force, with early recruits including Sir Christopher Wren, Pepys and

Milton, and the reigning monarch traditionally occupying the post of Captain General.

That said, the first named of these sadly played no part in the design of older Armoury House which, with its exploding cannonball decorations in place of urns, was built in 1735. The embattled gateway, shown here with its heavily martial rock finish, is of course more recent, having been added during Queen Victoria's reign, at which time the prefix 'Honourable' was finally confirmed, although it had been in casual use by the Company since at least 1685.

As well as retaining the right to march through the City with colours flying, drums beating and bayonets fixed, the Company's members enjoy the privilege of firing royal salutes from the Tower Battery, also of appearing with pikes and muskets at the Lord Mayor's Show and acting as guards of honour.

Somewhat less expected, however, is their unsung role in sporting history: their extensive parade ground and firing field paid host to the first great game of cricket ever staged. Kent took on All England here on 18 June 1744 – a full seventy years before Lord's was up and running. Interestingly, forty years later, the same site was also to be the launching point for the first 'aerial traveller in the English atmosphere' when, on 15 September 1784, Vincenzo Lunardi made an ascent from here in his balloon.

BLACKFRIARS STATION
QUEEN VICTORIA STREET, EC1

From Bromley to Bremen

Far from believing in the romance of travel, most people forced on to London's fragmenting transport network would presumably be content these days if the trains were simply clean, on time, safe and reliable.

Certainly, it comes as something of a surprise to discover within the City's unloveliest station evidence of an earlier age when this small corner of commuter London really did offer connections to some of the great cities of the world.

Built in 1886 and until 1937 called St Paul's station, Blackfriars had originally been part of the historic London, Chatham & Dover Railway at a time when international travel still held the promise of real adventure. As the company's London terminus, the small Italianate station had been constructed to connect no fewer than seven incoming lines with the District Railway, thereby giving LC&DR passengers easy access to other parts of the capital via the Metropolitan Railway.

With the seven lines carried over the Thames on one of Blackfriars' two splendid iron railway bridges – the eastern one, built by H.M. Brunel and J. Wolfe-Barry – those same passengers had the option to travel further afield, to which end they would have seen cut into the stone blocks of the original station entrance the names of several rather more exotic destinations including Brindisi on the Adriatic coast, Bremen, Marseilles and even St Petersburg.

Happily, the blocks in question are still there now, relocated inside the station during the 1977 rebuild. Here their almost comical incongruity is emphasised by other, more prosaic place names carved alongside, such as Bromley, Beckenham and Westgate-on-Sea.

If nothing else they speak volumes for the drive, bluster and sheer ambition of the LC&DR's chair-man, James Staats Forbes, who was to preside over London's District Railway for more than thirty years.

One of the real giants of the nineteenth-century railway age and something of a railway genius, he reportedly 'propounded his ideas with such vigour as to carry his shareholders with him regardless of whether his ideas were likely to be profitable or not'. But, perhaps unsurprisingly, he was also a complex and difficult character, and never more so than when faced with his old adversary Sir Edward Watkin, chairman of the rival Metropolitan Railway.

Their rivalry came to a head in the 1860s when Sir Joseph Bazalgette, of the Metropolitan Board of Works, required the two lines to link up to form the new Circle Line. Nothing, one would have thought, could have been more sensible or easier to achieve than running the District Line north for a few hundred yards at its eastern and western extremities, and the Metropolitan Line south at the same points to link up with it. But the two tycoons had different ideas about working together and, wholly against the public and shareholders' interest, Watkin and Forbes continued to fight it out for years and years.

As a result, by 1870 the two lines were more or less complete and less than a mile apart – the one stopping at Mansion House, the other at Tower Hill. Pathetically, it was to take nearly fourteen years to close the gap and complete the loop, the two men, compelled by government and public pressure, eventually relenting (just) and being persuaded, just once, to sit together on the inaugural run of London's newly completed Circle Line.

BUNHILL FIELDS
CITY ROAD, EC1

Bring Out Your Dead

A prehistoric burial ground known as the Bone Hill – and now the sole surviving City burial ground as distinct from a churchyard – one of the three great fields of Finsbury, became a dumping ground for cartloads of bones from the charnel house at St Paul's. Later, as 'the Cemetery of Puritan England', it was established as a place of more orderly interment for dissenters and other religious nonconformists.

Having leased the land since the early fourteenth century, the Corporation of London had in fact planned in the 1660s to use it as a place to bury the dead from the Great Plague. However, no evidence that they ever did so has come to light, nor more significantly has any documentation been produced proving that it was consecrated ground.

As a result, it was much favoured by religious nonconformists who – while it lacks any church buildings, although Wesley's famous chapel is opposite – were thus free to conduct funerals here and to bury their dead without reference to the *Book of Common Prayer*.

With the last such interment here made as long ago as January 1854, it has been a public open space since 1864 and as such provides a peaceful amenity for City workers. Nevertheless, it still gives one an excellent impression of how London's old burial grounds would have looked in the years before the search for space led to a move out of town in the mid-nineteenth century. Thus, in just 4 acres, with a spiked gate at one corner to thwart the efforts of the resurrection men, are crammed the remains and memorials of at least 120,000 individuals.

With their disorderly graves now crowded together beneath the spreading branches of mature plane, oak and lime trees, those in residence include Daniel Defoe, William Blake and his wife Catherine Sophia, John Bunyan, Susannah Wesley (mother of nineteen, including John and Charles) and Cromwell's son-in-law General Fleetwood. There are also at least two proper villains: Robert Tilling, who was executed for murdering his master in 1760; and the banker Henry Fauntleroy, who forged signatures, and scammed and squandered an incredible £250,000 (at nineteenth-century prices) before being hanged at Newgate Gaol.

Inevitably, there are some peculiarities here too. On Bunyan's memorial, for example, the recumbent figure is probably not Bunyan at all but rather a representation of the tomb's original incumbent, one John Strudwick. His effigy was added to the tomb in 1862 when, at the behest of the Earl of Shaftesbury, this was restored using funds raised by public subscription. Nearby is the tomb of John Lettsom, a physician who made his fortune in the West Indies before introducing the mangel-wurzel to England, and another for poor Dame Mary Page, widow of Sir Gregory Page Bt, who 'in 67 months was tapp'd 66 times and had taken away 240 gallons of water without ever repining for her case or fearing the operation'. It was, alas, all to no avail and she died, aged 56, in 1728.

ELY PLACE
CHARTERHOUSE STREET, EC1

Ancient Place of Sanctuary

In London's royal parks it is illegal for people in bath chairs to travel three abreast, or for anyone to touch a pelican without first obtaining written permission. Members of Parliament are forbidden to attend the House of Commons dressed in a suit of armour. Cabbies are similarly required to carry 'sufficient foodstuffs for the horse' – hence the vacant space next to the driver of a classic black cab, large enough for a bale of hay – and to answer the call of nature 'only against the rear of the vehicle, and in a seemly fashion', although he or she is permitted to ask a passing police constable to shield them with his cape while so engaged.

Occasionally, however, these arcane laws can work to the transgressor's advantage, so that, for example, anyone falling foul of one could do worse than run to here. This is because, while abutting the City borders and clearly built on London soil, the elegant cul-de-sac known as Ely Place was for years technically a part of Cambridgeshire and as such was said to be off limits to the Met.

Certainly, it is still true that the police may pass by this charming little gate lodge and enter the street only if invited, though the likelihood is that this anomaly has more to do with it being Crown property than it having once been the London address of the powerful Bishops of Ely.

Originally the bishops had lodged at the Temple, until a row with the Knights Templar in about 1290 forced them to move on. Around this date the incumbent had his own house built here and this, with a few interruptions, remained in use until 1772 when the bishops moved again, this time to Dover Street in Mayfair.

John of Gaunt lived here for a while too, after his fabulous Savoy Palace was destroyed in the Peasants' Revolt. And in 1531 Ely House played host to an immense five-day banquet for Henry VIII and Catherine of Aragon, at which were consumed 100 sheep, 51 cows, 24 oxen, 91 pigs, 444 pigeons, 168 swans, 720 chickens and a staggering 4,000 larks.

Five hundred years later, the house, sadly, has gone but this is still a curious and charming by way. The little pre-Reformation church of St Etheldreda, for example, is the oldest Catholic church in the capital, having at one time been the chapel and crypt of the bishop's palace.

Further along, opposite No. 33, a small, dark passage gives on to Hatton Garden, passing on its way what may well be London's least public public house. Appropriately called the Ye Old Mitre, the original having been built by Bishop Goodrich in 1546 for his servants, the present building (if you can find it) dates only from 1772. It houses an old stump of a cherry tree around which the young Elizabeth I is said to have danced with her future Chancellor – Sir Christopher Hatton, hence Hatton Garden – the Queen having forced her Lord Bishop to lease part of his garden to her favourite at a rent of £10 a year, ten loads of hay and a rose picked at midsummer.

GATEHOUSE
ST BARTHOLOMEW'S HOSPITAL, EC1

Diseased Beggars Welcome

London's oldest hospital, Bart's, was built at a time when Death really did stalk the streets of London. With harsh and unsanitary living conditions, and successive waves of plague or worse, the average life expectancy in twelfth-century London may have been a tad better than at the Conquest but it was still, clearly, brutally short.

Reliable figures sadly do not exist, but it is thought that in the City's poorer districts twenty to twenty-five years would have been reasonable for a man, while the rich probably enjoyed a mere ten-year advantage. The absence of anything that could reasonably be described as medical science also meant that, for the sick, hope and expectation were rarely the same thing, so a smart new monastic hospital on the edge of the City was clearly something to be welcomed. That said, with only a master, eight brethren and four Augustinian nuns on the staff, the sick were only ever promised 'diligence and care in all gentleness'.

Like any great city, and at the time there was none greater than this, London was no stranger to sickness, disease and epidemics. Rapid population increases inevitably brought with them issues of public health, and by 1547 Bart's – having survived the Reformation (Henry VIII signed the necessary documents less than a fortnight before his death) – was taking in hundreds of 'diseased beggars' as well as the orphans and needy who had previously been its chief concern.

The care offered was naturally extremely primitive: at this time, it was still considered good practice to put the bodies of mice into surgical wounds, and rat dung was thought to be a good cure for falling hair. Indeed, it was to be another 100 years or so before any actual medical students arrived at the hospital, and until as late as 1699 surgeons here were still obliged to obtain the permission of unqualified, lay governors before performing any actual procedures – a bid, clearly, to ensure none of them fraudulently obtained the 6s 8d they were due for each amputation by carrying out any unnecessary operations.

The cheerful little Gatehouse shown here dates from just after this time; however, the eighteenth century saw extensive rebuilding on the site, with the result that today visitors to the hospital can see several fine Georgian buildings by James Gibbs, George Dance the Younger, and Thomas and Philip Hardwick.

That said, having been designed in 1702 by Edward Strong and surmounted by a statue of Henry VIII caught in a characteristic pose by Francis Bird, the structure was actually rebuilt in 1834. Happily, though, while incorporating a sequence of rooms above it, Philip Hardwick maintained much of the style and scale of the original. Accordingly, when viewed from West Smithfield today, the stone gateway looks for all the world like the entrance to one of the Oxford colleges. Like those, it is ignored by most people hurrying along the pavement, but for anyone who cares to glance up it is both a striking and well-proportioned little composition.

GREY FRIARS MONASTERY
NEWGATE STREET, EC1

Lost Royal Tombs

The burial place of three queens and the heart of a fourth, the first church on this site was originally part of a monastery, built in 1225 by the first group of Franciscan or 'Grey Friars' to arrive in England.

The group of just four soon grew to eighty, their simple life and good works among the poor rapidly attracting the patronage of many admirers both rich and royal. One early benefactor was the Sheriff of London, John Travers, who presented the order with a house on Cornhill. Shortly thereafter, a City mercer called John Ewin gave it a parcel of land in Stinking Lane – aptly named as it was close to the abattoirs – and the monastic estate grew from there. Then, in 1291, the heart of Eleanor of Provence, wife of Henry III, was buried within the precincts, underlining a royal connection which was to endure.

Less than twenty years later, Queen Margaret set about rebuilding the church, the second wife of Edward I dying before the work was completed and being buried in front of the high altar. Upon completion in 1348, however, it was a truly massive structure, an overall length of 300ft making it second only in the City to St Paul's Cathedral and as such almost certainly the largest church in the kingdom.

With a roll of benefactors that came to include Edward III's Queen Philippa, the monastery and its church soon became a highly fashionable place to be interred. Many of the noble dead were buried in monk's garb in order to speed their route to Heaven, and within ten years yet another queen was laid to rest here. This time it was Isabella, Thomas Gray's reviled 'She-wolf of France' who married Edward II but subsequently, with her lover Roger Mortimer, Earl of March, had him murdered. Four years later she was joined by her daughter, Joan de la Tour, Queen of Scotland.

In all some 663 nobles were buried here, but following the Dissolution the majority of their tombs and memorials were sold for a paltry £50; in 1547 the monks' chapel was combined with the nearby St Nicholas by the Shambles to become the new parish church of Christ Church.

Together with a library presented by Sir Dick Whittington in 1425 (and containing books estimated at the time to be worth a handsome £400), Christ Church was reduced to ruins in the Great Fire. Wren was commissioned to build a replacement, in part following the ground plan of the original, which became very much one of his most expensive schemes; a steeple was finally added in 1704.

Unfortunately, this incarnation was similarly doomed and fell to enemy action in 1940, together with some reportedly beautiful choir stalls constructed using timber from an Armada warship. Today all that remains is the tower, one of Wren's best, together with an avenue of trees marking the position of the nave.

POSTMAN'S PARK
LITTLE BRITAIN, EC1

A Modest Valhalla

Pavement-shuffling during the sales, or stranded bus to bumper in the evening rush hour, it may not seem like it but London is still one of the greenest cities in the world. This is not simply because of what Prime Minister Pitt famously described in *Hansard* on 30 June 1808 as 'the lungs of London' – the more than 6,000 acres of Epping Forest on the one side, and on the other that great arc of historic parks and gardens at Bushy and Hampton Court, Syon, Osterley, Richmond and Kew. Nor, indeed, is it just down to the well-known cultivated wildernesses of Hampstead Heath and Hyde Park, the latter a particularly surprising survivor as it occupies 340 acres of some of the most valuable real estate on the planet. Rather it is because it has so many lesser-known green spaces, literally hundreds of them: the railed-in shrubberies of scores of Georgian and Victorian squares, the tranquil walks and gardens along parts of the Thames, and of course those hidden enclaves which make up the lawyers' ancient Inns of Court – the gates barred shut each evening but during the day open for anyone to enjoy.

Some of the nicest, it is true, are still off-limits. Between Pall Mall and Piccadilly, for example, the shuttered doors of clubland conceal elegant courtyards and gardens in which liveried servants still serve sundowners to the fortunate few. In Belgravia and Chelsea, on land held for generations by successive dukes of Westminster and Cadogan earls, only residents can avail themselves of the leafy garden squares (Vincent Square near Victoria station is similarly reserved for Westminster's schoolboy cricketers). And, of course, at the top of the Mall is London's largest private garden: 40 high-walled acres or so, complete with a lake, rare shrubs including a mulberry tree planted by James I, flamingos and who knows what else for Her Majesty to enjoy.

But glancing at a street map it is clear that there are plenty of others to choose from. Some large, some small, some the surviving fragments of ancient royal hunting grounds, others offering a quick escape from the crowded streets of the Square Mile, the hurly-burly and the breathless pace of modern urban life.

Of these, peaceful Postman's Park is one of the most delightful and unexpected. So called because of its proximity to the old General Post Office building behind St Paul's, it couldn't provide a stronger contrast to its hard-faced high-rise neighbours. Naturally popular with City workers who come to kick off their shoes and share their sandwiches with the pigeons, it is where the celebrated Victorian painter G.F. Watts (1817–1904) proposed siting a national and, as it turned out, quite heart-rending memorial to the heroism of ordinary men, women and, especially, children.

Briefly married to the actress Ellen Terry, he had in mind otherwise unsung heroes like Alice Ayres, 'daughter of a bricklayer's labourer, who by intrepid conduct saved three children from a burning house at the cost of her own young life'; Thomas Simpson, who 'died of exhaustion after saving many lives from the breaking ice at Highgate Ponds'; and Harry Sisley of Kilburn, who was just 10 years old when in 1878 he drowned attempting to rescue his baby brother. The idea caught on, but only briefly, and following the death of Watts and his second wife no more plaques were added to their touching collection of fifty-three until 2009, when Leigh Pitt, a print technician who died saving a 9-year-old boy from drowning, was added. Pitt was the first new addition in seventy-eight years.

ST BARTHOLOMEW THE GREAT
WEST SMITHFIELD, EC1

London's Oldest Church

Together with its splendid Tudor gatehouse, the oldest church in the capital is in reality the last surviving portion of an Augustinian priory founded in 1123 by Rahere, sometime jester at the court of Henry I.

Encouraged by his patron, the Bishop of London, Rahere had become a monk and later a prebendary to St Paul's. But in about 1120, he contracted malaria during a pilgrimage to Rome and while ill experienced a vision of St Bartholomew rescuing him from a winged monster. Immediately afterwards he made a vow that if he recovered and returned to England safely he would found a hospital 'yn recreacion of poure men'.

In a second vision, St Bartholomew is said to have made a gesture towards the area of Smithfield to the north of the City, so Rahere (the name is of Frankish origin) set about reclaiming some unpromising marshland on which to build his new foundation. First to be built was the hospital – modern-day Bart's, of course (see p. 47) – and then the priory, for which Rahere as its first prior built a choir, an ambulatory and a lady chapel.

In 1133, his former master granted Rahere and his canons the right to hold Bartholomew Fair on the property, which in its day proved a great source of wealth as the greatest cloth fair in the country. It is said that Rahere would occasionally perform his old juggling tricks there too, and indeed the fair remained a place of great entertainment until being suppressed by the authorities in 1855 when they tired of the regular public disorders with which it was associated.

Rahere finally died in 1144, but his church continued to grow, extended by several of his successors who added transepts, a crossing and a long nave – the timbered gateway marks the position of the south door. Eventually some 300ft in length, in 1539 it was surrendered to Henry VIII, the nave was pulled down and exactly 400 years after the death of Rahere the monastic buildings were sold on to Sir Richard Rich.

Mary I allowed some Dominicans to return in 1556, but three years later they were expelled by Elizabeth I and new uses were found for the buildings. The crypt was used as a coal bunker, then a wine store with hops in the sacristy; the lady chapel became a printer's workshop – Benjamin Franklin worked there in 1725 – and horses were stabled in the cloister.

In fact, it was not until the 1860s, when the Rich family sold up, that St Bartholomew's received the respect it was due. That was when the great Sir Aston Webb (1849–1930) began to restore the church – a sensitively handled project which took him twenty years or more – and in 1893 the adjacent porch as well.

Jumbled yet hugely atmospheric, the results may be a bit of a mishmash architecturally, but the place is still packed with delightful features. These include Rahere's sixteenth-century tomb, London's oldest wooden door, and an outstanding collection of Tudor and Jacobean memorials. Indeed, with the sole exception of the White Tower, St Bartholomew's is today the most impressive Norman survivor in central London.

WATCH HOUSE
GILTSPUR STREET, EC1

A Grim Reminder

Until the Anatomy Act of 1832, the only bodies to which the burgeoning medical profession could gain access were those of convicted murderers, the unfortunate corpses of whom were released into the custody of the barber-surgeons for dissection immediately after they had felt the full force of the law.

Before this date, however, and as a direct consequence of the rapid progress being made in the medical sciences, there was an almost permanent imbalance in the equation of supply and demand. The number of murderers convicted by the courts, while considerable, was simply never sufficient to meet the call for bodies, as a result of which (and with increasingly high prices being paid for suitable cadavers) churches and graveyards were routinely being plundered for fresh supplies.

As this ghoulish practice became rife, tombs across the country were railed in or otherwise made safe, gates were barricaded or spiked (see p. 44) and many churches were even forced to build special watch houses in order to more effectively protect their dead.

Few of these now survive in London – there is another attached to St Clement Danes in the Strand – but this one dating from 1792 is in good shape. One can be sure it would have been much needed too, since, with the great St Bartholomew's Hospital just across the road, there would always have been plenty of local demand here for fresh, newly buried bodies.

In fact, as part of the Church of Holy Sepulchre-without-Newgate (otherwise known as St Sepulchre's) this particular watch house is doubly grisly, as for years it was closely associated with the notoriously grim gaol of the same name.

Here the tradition was that the death-cart hauling condemned men from Newgate to Tyburn – typically after a trial lasting barely fifteen minutes – would halt outside St Sepulchre's in order that the prisoners could be presented with a nosegay. Worse still, and for the best part of a century and a half, a bequest made to the church in 1605 paid for a bellman to leave the church for the gaol on the night before each execution.

After solemnly ringing his handbell, he would recite the following to the joy of bystanders:

> All you that in the condemned hold do lie,
> Prepare you, for tomorrow you shall die;
> Watch all and pray, the hour is drawing near
> That before the Almighty you must appear;
> Examine well yourselves, in time repent,
> That you may not to eternal flames be sent:
> And when St Sepulchre's bell tomorrow tolls,
> The Lord above have mercy on your souls.

More cheerfully remembered these days as the bells of Old Bailey in the children's rhyme 'Oranges and Lemons', the actual execution bell now resides in a glass case to the south of the nave.

GRESHAM COLLEGE
BARNARD'S INN, EC2

Memorial Lectures 400 Years On

Established in the year of his death by Sir Thomas Gresham (*c.* 1519–79), builder of the Royal Exchange, for more than four centuries the college has presented a series of free public lectures, delivered by its own distinguished panel of Gresham professors, of whom Sir Christopher Wren was one. Conceived to convey to the lay population something of the glories and new learning of the Renaissance, the daily lectures were intended to advance understanding of divinity, music, astronomy, geometry, law, physics and rhetoric.

The son of Lord Mayor Sir Richard Gresham, Sir Thomas served as Edward VI's agent in Antwerp. Significantly, he retained this prestigious position throughout Mary's reign too, and for the first nine years of Queen Elizabeth's. Extremely rich as a result, until 1768 the college found a home in his own fine mansion in Bishopsgate.

Standing for more than two centuries and described by John Stow as 'the most spacious of all there about', it was here that the seven professors, each paid £50 a year, delivered their lectures. Their salaries were paid using revenue from the rents on shops around the Royal Exchange, this having been bequeathed in equal halves to the Mercers' Company and the City Corporation. From 1662 to 1710, the Royal Society for the Advancement of Natural Science met in the house too, having developed from discussions between those same professors.

Surviving the Great Fire, unlike so many of the great houses, Gresham's house was nevertheless eventually demolished and from 1768 the college met in a room above the Royal Exchange, until finally securing its own premises in Gresham Street in 1842. In 1991, however, it moved again, to this building: Barnard's Inn Hall.

By this time an eighth, more contemporary subject had been added to the curriculum – Commerce – but there was nothing newfangled about the premises. A former Inn of Chancery affiliated to Gray's Inn, Barnard's Inn was described by Dickens in *Great Expectations* but was first recorded as part of the estate of Sir Adam de Basyng, Mayor of London, in 1252. It was acquired by the Mercers in the late nineteenth century, the company paying £43,000 for the freehold and using the buildings for its school until this closed in 1959.

The hall now used by the college dates from the late fourteenth century and, built as part of what would have been a great medieval house, has some fine early sixteenth-century linen-fold panels with Renaissance motifs. But one portion of the southern wall of the Council Chamber (situated below the hall) is clearly much older and dates from the Roman period.

Badly damaged in 1780 during the Gordon Riots, the hall has been carefully restored more recently. This has revealed some real treasures, including the old roof timbers (with an original, octagonal louvred 'fumer' or smoke vent) and two transverse frames, apparently pairs of base crucks with tie beams, which support a crown-post and collar purlin roof, thought to be the last surviving examples in Greater London.

THE MONUMENT
FISH STREET HILL, EC2

Doric Laboratory

The same Act which provided for the rebuilding of the City after the Great Fire also required that a 'Column or Pillar of Brace or Stone be erected on or neere unto the place where the said Fire soe unhappily began'.

Almost inevitably it fell to Wren to come up with a design, and, with his close friend and fellow scientist Robert Hooke, he proposed several ideas including, most radically, a perforated column topped by a phoenix and with bronze flames leaping through the holes.

In the event, the King and the Corporation opted for something simpler, namely this enormous, hollow Roman Doric column to commemorate the devastation of 373 City acres, and a further 63 beyond the walls, including the destruction of St Paul's Cathedral and another eighty-four churches.

In fact, the design for what is still the world's tallest free-standing stone column is generally now recognised as being Hooke's not Wren's, the former's diary making reference to his model of the 'piller' in October 1673. But how many visitors today, one wonders, realise that he didn't make it hollow simply to accommodate a spiral staircase rising to the flaming urn at the top. In fact, he and Wren, both keen astronomical observers, were hoping to mount a giant zenith telescope inside it, similar to the one Hooke had previously run through his house at Gresham College.

Hooke's wish was to use the instrument to observe the so-called stellar parallax, an experiment requiring a chosen star to be observed twice in the same position exactly six months apart. Unfortunately, the Gresham telescope had proved too unstable; so too did the new 202ft Monument.

His attempts to combine architecture and science in this way were far from new – before the Fire he had worked with pendulums at the old St Paul's – but neither were they entirely fruitless. We know this because the same diary refers to work with a mercury barometer at the 'Fish Street Piller' on 16 May 1678. Exactly a week later, Hooke recorded an 'experiment at Column. Lent Mr Hunt a cylinder to do it,' and, a week after that, the minutes of the Royal Society make reference to his measuring the air pressure as he descended the Monument steps.

Wren too found this idea appealing, offsetting the huge cost of new buildings by designing them in such a way that they could double as scientific laboratories. As a result, his design for the Society's new home on the site of the Earl of Arundel's Renaissance-style 'museum garden' incorporated a long gallery 'for the tryal of glasses & other experiments that require length'. In 1704, he also proposed building the south-west staircase of his new St Paul's in such a manner as to provide a suitable mount for the 123ft tubeless telescope presented to the Society by the younger Constantijn Huygens in 1692.

Sadly, neither plan came to fruition. As a result, the Monument – retaining its dignity if not its dominance, and while handsomely preserving 'the memory of this dreadful Visitation' – now stands as a unique reminder of this early flowering of the scientific revolution.

ROMAN WALL
TOWER HILL, EC3

Built to Last

Surprisingly extensive remains of a 2-mile Roman wall can be still seen here by the Tower, at the Barbican and on London Wall, in Crutched Friars and elsewhere, these having survived in large part because later builders (while naturally keen to salvage any useful building materials) were simply unable to demolish such substantial masonry.

The walls themselves were built late in the second century using Kentish ragstone brought in barges up the Medway, along the coast and into the Thames. One such barge, some 52ft long and nearly 20 wide, had the misfortune to sink at its moorings; after being excavated in 1962–63 at a site close to Blackfriars Bridge the remains were removed to the Museum of London.

Eventually enclosing more than 300 acres, the wall would have been 18ft high when completed, 6 to 9ft wide, and topped by a walkway and parapet. Built on to a pre-existing Roman fort close to modern Wood Street – thereby explaining the irregular shape of the medieval city – it incorporated eight gates, more than twenty defensive bastions or towers and a defensive ditch on the outer side.

Work on the wall is known to have continued right up until Rome's withdrawal from Britain in AD 410, and it was still substantially intact in 457 when it formed a crucial part of London's defences against marauding Saxons. Similarly, as late as the sixteenth century, the ditch was being used as a dump for domestic waste (including, it is said, dead dogs) by which time and throughout the City many parts of the walls had been used as foundations for newer buildings with successive courses of medieval and later brickwork being built on top of it.

Some salvage efforts were clearly successful: at the Church of All Hallows by the Tower, for instance, an arch clearly of Saxon form has just as clearly been built using Roman bricks. But elsewhere the Roman work has proved sufficiently enduring, and its fine and robust construction can still be discerned. Examples of this can be seen here close to Tower Hill Underground station at 8–10 Cooper's Row and in the churchyard of St Alfege's.

Strange apsidal ends have also been discovered in the cellars of several nineteenth-century warehouses, their builders having been forced to accommodate stubborn Roman structures which proved completely resistant to removal. More recent builders have made similar discoveries – for example at Crosswall, in Lime Street and in Pudding Lane – although these sites, while carefully documented at the time and preserved, are sadly now lost to view.

ROYAL MINT
TOWER HILL, EC3

A Thousand Years of Making Money

Founded as long ago as AD 825, and with a secret tunnel through to St Katherine's Dock, London's Royal Mint only closed in 1980, by which time all its operations had moved to Llantrisant in South Wales.

Its proximity to the Tower is not coincidental, as the right of coinage had been a royal prerogative since the concept of money arrived here with the Romans. Thus, by 1279, the Mint was operating between the inner and outer walls of the Tower, an official Master of the Mint exercising control over design, dies and overall quality of the finished product on behalf of the monarch. Most famously, Sir Isaac Newton held this post from 1699 to 1727, but by 1870 the role had been abolished and the responsibilities devolved on to the Chancellor of the Exchequer.

Even basing the Mint in the Tower, however, failed to prevent at least one successful armed robbery: in 1798 some 2,805 guineas – perhaps £1 million at today's values – were stolen and the staff held at gunpoint. Not long afterwards, with the country at war with France and the garrison demanding more space, the decision was taken to move operations outside the walls.

This suited the officers of the Mint too, who wished to install larger, steam-powered machinery, and soon new buildings were designed by James Johnson in a sombre if fashionable neo-Classical style. The work was completed after his death by Sir Robert Smirke, with the first coins being struck here in April 1810 and the keys of the old Tower Mint being returned to the Constable in August 1812.

'Dull' or 'of modest grandeur', depending on whose opinion one listened to, the new buildings were on a site only recently vacated by tobacco warehouses and a ship's biscuit factory, and before this an apparently unexceptional Cistercian abbey, St Mary Graces, founded by Edward III in 1349.

With the main quadrangle flanked by two gatehouses, buildings housing the coin-making machinery soon shared the site with accommodation blocks for officers and staff. The whole complex was surrounded by a boundary wall and walkway patrolled by soldiers from the Mint's own military guard.

With new technology coming on stream all the time, however, and electric power eventually replacing steam, the factory buildings were repeatedly renewed as the Mint struggled to keep pace with demand both from home and abroad. By the 1960s, little remained of the original structure besides Smirke's work and the gatehouses in front. Thereafter, with the demands of decimalisation looming, the logical transfer out of central London began.

Shortly afterwards, and to great excitement all round, workmen restoring St Katherine's Dock uncovered what appeared to be a secret tunnel linking the dock to the Mint walls. At first thought to be evidence of yet another elaborate attempt to rob the Mint but, upon closer examination, it sadly proved to be simply evidence of a feasibility study to examine the possibility of constructing a pedestrian underpass beneath East Smithfield.

DISUSED TUNNELS
KING WILLIAM STREET, EC4

Reminders of Metropolitan Moles

Given the expense and complexities involved in their construction, the sheer number of tunnels excavated under London and then hastily abandoned comes as something of a surprise.

At Woolwich in south-east London, for example, the former Royal Arsenal had its own underground railway system with tunnels dating back to 1716. (Running from Shooters Hill to unlovely Thamesmead, when it was no longer required by the military it was taken over and used as temporary storage by the British Library.) Not far away, in Greenwich Park, a much older network of apparently medieval conduits, each one brick-lined and large enough to walk through, stretches out beneath Sir Christopher Wren's old Royal Observatory. And then of course there's the Kingsway Underpass (see p. 22).

Perhaps the most astonishing realisation, however, is just how many disused tunnels there are actually running under the Thames. In fact, the capital has more tunnels under her principal river than any other city in the world (twenty all told between Hammersmith and Tilbury). Not that their number in any way diminishes the really considerable engineering challenges their construction represented in their day, nor the impression of waste suggested by their subsequent abandonment.

Typical is the tunnel which runs from the crumbling power station at Battersea across to Dolphin Square and the Churchill Gardens Estate, the residents of which once enjoyed central heating courtesy of scalding water piped across the Thames. But rather larger is the so-called Charing Cross Loop, which used to form part of the Northern Line, and then further downriver two more redundant tunnels, which were once used to ferry the same line across from Stockwell through London Bridge station to the long-abandoned King William Street station by the Monument.

Once the northern terminus of the City & South London Railway – famously the world's first Tube line – this was opened by the Prince of Wales in 1890 and was originally designed for cable-hauled rather than electric locomotives. It closed less than ten years later, however, at which time, when proposals were invited for its future use, the applicants included a farmer who planned to use the subterranean space to grow mushrooms.

Away from the river, there is another abandoned Tube line too, this one running from Smithfield to St Pancras and formerly part of the Metropolitan Line, and also the so-called 'mail rail', the Post Office's famous subterranean link from Paddington to Whitechapel that has only recently been decommissioned.

Completed in 1927 – work had begun in 1913 but was interrupted by the First World War, when the 9ft-diameter tunnels were used to store the Elgin Marbles – this unique line once boasted eight stations and driverless trains capable of carrying up to half a ton of mail at 35mph. Originally there were to be many more of these, with several branch lines connecting to sorting offices north and south of the river, in effect creating a second, mini Circle Line. But sadly these were never completed. Instead, today there are two short, blind tunnels running north-west off the main line at Mount Pleasant and south-east from Holborn. Their future, like that of the rest of the line, is at present uncertain.

LONDON STONE
CANNON STREET, EC4

Measuring the Miles

For years set into a niche within the wall of a Chinese bank, but originally on the other side of the street where (until this was bombed in 1941) it was placed against the wall of Wren's curious St Swithin's Church, this mysterious lump of London masonry has been in the City since at least 1198.

What lies behind the hideous grille, a piece of Clipsham limestone or oolite, is therefore one of London's very oldest landmarks. Even so, weathered but otherwise unmarked except for a pair of grooves in its round-shouldered top, the precise origins of the so-called *lonenstan* remain frustratingly obscure.

Since the sixteenth century, for example, the idea has taken root that it is a Roman milestone, the milestone indeed from which all measurements in Britannia were taken. But other authorities think it has a Druidic connection, suggesting that it sits on a ley line connecting significant places, that it marks the mystical centre point of London or even the British Isles, or that it once formed part of a stone circle associated with King Lud (hence Lud's Town or London, Ludgate and so on).

The Roman theory, however, is supported by the 1961 discovery of remains beneath nearby Cannon Street station, which for some while were thought to be of sufficient grandeur (and suitably placed) to be the governor's palace. It is known too that during the reign of Augustus an order went out for a central stone to be set up in the Forum in Rome, 8ft tall and covered in gilt bronze, marking the starting point for measurement of the Roman highways. As Constantine is known to have installed something similar in Byzantium, it seems plausible that once London was confirmed as the chief city of the province of Britannia it too might have had its own *milliarium aureum*, or golden milestone.

That said, there are no contemporary references to any such stone or monument. Indeed, the earliest mention unearthed by Stow is only from the tenth century, found in a book belonging to the Saxon King Athelstan which refers to rents from places 'near unto London stone'. Interestingly the name of the City's first mayor contains a similar reference: Henry Fitz-Ailwin de Londonestone, meaning Henry, son of Ailwin of London Stone, who was appointed to the post some time before 1193.

But, whatever its origins, it has certainly been an important landmark for many centuries, a place where oaths were sworn, proclamations made, even, it has been suggested, laws passed. It is known too that during Jack Cade's rebellion in 1450, the rebel calling himself John Mortimer arrived here from Kent to protest about the King's taxes. Objecting to the extortion, he struck this very stone with his sword declaring himself to be 'lord of this city'.

His rebellion failed, of course, its leaders made subject to the gruesome 'Harvest of the Heads'. But thanks to Shakespeare the scene lives on in *Henry VI*, *Part 2*:

> Here, sitting upon London-stone, I charge and command that, of the city's cost, the pissing-conduit run nothing but claret wine this first year of our reign. And now henceforward it shall be treason for any that calls me other than Lord Mortimer.

MIDDLE AND INNER TEMPLE
FLEET STREET, EC4

Perfect Metaphor for the Profession

Secretive, historic and hidebound – any such description of the connected enclaves of Middle and Inner Temple could just as accurately be applied to the profession they serve. They take their name from the twelfth-century Knights Templar, who built their famous Round Church here (as a copy of Jerusalem's Holy Sepulchre), together with a magnificent monastery. With the suppression of the powerful order by Clement V in 1312, and later of the Knights Hospitallers of St John of Jerusalem, their property reverted to the Crown.

In 1609, however, it was granted by James I to the Hospitallers' tenants, the lawyers or Benchers, which is to say the senior qualified members of the two Inns of Court. Calling themselves the Societies of the Middle and Inner Temple – the formal, physical division between the two didn't take place until 1732 – they were obliged to maintain the church but soon set about developing the other buildings to suit their own purposes. This meant building halls, libraries and dwelling places, each arranged in a complex honeycomb around the old knights' deserted quarters.

Access to the lawyers' warren nowadays is easy, via one of several lanes on the south side of Fleet Street between Bouverie and Essex Street, or from the Embankment. On foot, the most evocative way in, however, is through the stone gateway giving on to Inner Temple Lane, an authentic survivor of the Great Fire and surmounted by the City's only complete and remaining timber-framed Jacobean townhouse.

James Boswell was a great one for walking the streets, and after nearly 250 years his description of this place still, incredibly, rings true:

> A most agreeable place [he called it]. You quit all the hurry and bustle of the City in Fleet Street and the Strand, and all at once find yourself in a pleasant, academical retreat. You see good convenient buildings, handsome walks, you view the silver Thames. You are shaded by venerable trees. Crows are cawing above your head.

Sadly, these days students of the law no longer get to live and sleep here as they once did. But as a nod to the residential tradition, would-be barristers are still formally required to keep terms by dining in Hall at least three times each term before being called to the Bar – in addition to passing the necessary examinations, of course.

The most important thing for the visitor, however, is to take one's time in exploring the various little courtyards and walkways. Some of the architecture, is inevitably bogus, as the area was heavily bombed in the 1940s. But King's Bench Walk (by Wren) is delightful, the ancient Round Church quite haunting and, while the reconstructed Middle Temple Hall (1562–70) may not be as old as its Lincoln's Inn rival, with its massive, double hammerbeam roof it is certainly far grander. Together with the late seventeenth-century New Court, the mellow brickwork and quiet fountains, the expansive gardens spreading down to the river and of course the enviable absence of traffic, the whole area still gives a perfect impression of a secluded, privileged and highly prized little village.

MITHRAEUM
12 WALBROOK, EC4N

Roman Temple to a Persian God

London's famous Temple of Mithras was first revealed only as a result of enemy action during the Second World War. At that time, a plan was devised to better understand the development of Londinium and the medieval settlements by cutting a series of trenches across bomb sites in the City.

With up to a third of the area within the line of the Roman wall devastated by the Blitz, it was clearly an opportunity too good to miss. Inevitably the strictures of post-war austerity would limit the scale of the work which could be undertaken, but at the same time the newly formed Roman and Medieval Excavation Council – a joint project carried out under the auspices of the Society of Antiquaries and the London Museum – recognised that substantial portions of the historical City were now laid bare, many of them for the first time in centuries.

In all, some fifty-three sites were excavated by the Council from 1947 to 1962: its discoveries over this period including a hitherto unknown fort at Cripplegate, an important quay at Pudding Lane near Billingsgate and London's first wooden bridge across the Thames. The best known, however, is the one whose outline can still be seen at pavement level. When it was excavated in 1954 it was in the full glare of national publicity, with at times up to 30,000 Londoners looking on.

Dating from around AD 240, the existence of the temple was first suspected as long ago as 1889 when a relief showing the god Mithras ritually slaying a bull was discovered in the Walbrook along with a sculpture of a reclining river god; both are now in the Museum of London. The relief was dedicated to Ulpius Silvanus, a veteran of a 2nd Legion of Augustus. This confirmed suspicions about the temple since, when it spread from Persia, the worship of this 'god of the Unconquered Sun' is known to have developed into a potent, all-male cult which was particularly popular among soldiers and successful merchants.

The excavations themselves were carried out under the supervision of the Council's director, Professor W.F. Grimes, and revealed a temple that, in its day, would have been larger and of far greater splendour than most of its rivals. That said, its plan is not unlike an early Christian church. With an apse at its western end to house the altar, and pillars dividing the nave from two aisles, the building would have been kept dark to remind initiates that it was in a cave that Mithras slew the sacred bull from whose blood all life flowed.

Secretive and extremely exclusive, membership of the cult required applicants to pass through a series of harsh physical and mental ordeals. Thereafter only a life of abstinence, obedience, courage, fortitude and vigilance would enable them to rise through all seven grades of initiation. Members – many of them almost certainly officers stationed at the aforementioned fort – were also charged with keeping secret the mysteries of the cult by closely guarding them from outsiders.

SPANISH AND PORTUGUESE SYNAGOGUE
BEVIS MARKS, EC4

Three Centuries of Anglo-Jewry

Britain's oldest synagogue – though actually the second to be established by the Jews when they were readmitted following their expulsion in 1290 by Edward I – this is the most tangible reminder that the Jewish community has far deeper roots in English soil than might otherwise be supposed.

The majority of Jews in the country today are, of course, refugees, or descendants of refugees, from Tsarist and Nazi persecution, which is to say that they are relatively recent arrivals.

But, coming mainly from settlements in Normandy, Jews were already well established here in the twelfth century, with the largest numbers based in London and Norwich, and other relatively wealthy communities in York, Winchester and Canterbury, also in Oxford, where Great Jewry Street and Little Jewry Lane denote the areas settled by rich and poor Jews respectively.

They were repeatedly subject to slander, however, along with unfounded allegations of ritual murder and eventually, in York, Lincoln and elsewhere, large-scale massacres. The medieval population of around 5,000 had halved by the end of the thirteenth century when Edward took steps to expel them.

By the fifteenth century, the atmosphere had clearly improved slightly, sufficiently for a handful to settle in London after being exiled from Spain during the Inquisition in 1492. But only with the arrival of Cromwell – who reportedly used Jewish agents in matters of both espionage and diplomacy – and the establishment of the Commonwealth in 1649 did Jews arrive in substantial numbers.

Bevis Marks dates back to that era, specifically to 1701, by which time the community of Sephardic Jews for whom it was built had been established for nearly half a century in nearby Creechurch Lane.

Architecturally, it is not at all dissimilar to many other places of worship of the period; indeed both the layout and the fittings are much like those of many City churches. The chandeliers are notable, however, having been sent from Amsterdam where Rabbi Menassah ben Israel had been forceful in the campaign for the right for Jews to be allowed to resettle in England. One of the main support beams was presented to the community by Queen Anne, recognition perhaps that, while it was to be another 150 years before the Jews' full emancipation, the Establishment at least acknowledged the key role this community now played in the commercial life of the nation.

In Anne's own time, for example, the Menassah Lopes family proved invaluable in maintaining the financial stability of the City, a service repeated by the Salvadors during the reigns of George I, II and III. And in 1745, when the City was unsettled by reports of the Jacobite uprising, it was another member of this community, Samson Gideon (later Lord Earley, 1699–1762) who raised a phenomenal £1.7 million to help the government quell the panic in the markets and restore calm.

The synagogue's most famous sons, however, are Benjamin Disraeli, whose birth is recorded in its archives – his father Isaac d'Israeli was a devout member of the religious community – and David Salomans, who in 1855 became London's first ever Jewish Lord Mayor.

NORTH LONDON

CANONBURY TOWER
CANONBURY PLACE, N1

Freemasons' Miraculous Survivor

A tall Tudor tower, built on what are claimed to be pre-Roman foundations, the survival of Canonbury Tower would be surprising enough were Islington an isolated village in the country. The fact that it has survived intact and in an inner London borough makes it very special indeed.

Still attached to the ancient timbers and gabled rooms of Canonbury House, the tower is a remarkably well-preserved portion of a structure built for William Bolton, Prior of St Bartholomew during the reign of Henry VII. Confiscated during the Reformation, in the late sixteenth century this was transformed into a country residence for a rich cloth merchant called Sir John Spenser. Lord Mayor of London and a close friend of Sir Francis Bacon (1561–1626), Spenser left a rich interior – much of which still survives, including carved oak panelling and several fine fireplaces.

From his time, the tower has at least one romantic story attached to it, namely that in 1659 Sir John's daughter was lowered from the top in a basket in order to elope with the penniless Lord Compton. Today it is also something of a psychogeographer's dream dwelling, being thought not only to lie on at least two dozen different ley lines criss-crossing the capital, but also to have long and well-documented Masonic connections.

Much of the panelling and many of the plaster ceilings, for example, are said to incorporate secret Masonic and Rosicrucian symbols. Bacon – who in 1616 took a nine-year lease on the house from Lord Compton (the latter having succeeded in becoming Spenser's son-in-law) – has similarly been described as the 'Imperator of the Rosicrucian Order', although more objective historians maintain that the great polymath merely inspired various mysterious Masonic rituals rather than becoming an initiate himself.

Whatever the answer, Sir Francis is just one of several famous tower residents. The playwright Oliver Goldsmith was here too, taking some rooms from 1762 to 1764; also Ephraim Chambers, the creator of the eponymous *Cyclopaedia,* actually died in the tower in 1740; and later the American diplomat and man of letters Washington Irving (1783–1859).

More recently, however, and perhaps inspired by a lengthy reference to the place in a copy of *The Scientific Magazine and Freemasons' Repository* dated July 1797, the Masons have returned to the tower. With its 'quaint brickwork and funny little windows in the queerest places, from whence many of our past worthies looked forth', these days it is home to the Canonbury Masonic Research Centre, and this means – with the MRC being the venue for a series of public lectures 'presented by leading experts and scholars primarily concerned with issues relating to Freemasonry and allied traditions, mystical and esoteric traditions world-wide' – that for the first time in nearly 500 years the tower is at last relatively easy for the general public to visit.

HOLLY VILLAGE
SWAIN'S LANE, N6

Strictly Business not Benefaction

Another scheme initiated by the fantastically rich Baroness Burdett-Coutts, but not this time (as is often suggested) as a place to house her own domestic servants or staff recently retired from the family bank. Rather, a small but picturesque group of Grade II listed Gothic Revival cottages was built as a purely commercial venture, the cottages being let out to paying tenants on the usual basis and at reportedly very substantial rents.

Clustered in a pleasantly random way around another miniature village green – just one of many reasons why they are still highly sought after, as an alternative to a conventional London street – the contrast with her development for the poor of east London could not be more marked.

Here the style may be Gothic again, and the architect the same Henry Darbishire, but Holly Village is built on a far homelier scale than Columbia Market and Columbia Square (see p. 204). With more attractive and far more complex decoration, the whole has been carefully blended in with this leafier environment, whereas in the East End the Baroness's architect simply swept away everything which was there before.

That said, some of the detailing here is quite wild and the more you study it the stranger it becomes, with decorative motif piled upon motif in a manner which close to looks almost comically Victorian. Indeed, while Holly Village was very much at the vanguard of building design when it was completed in 1864, today one is scarcely surprised to find at least one architectural

academic dismissing the entire ensemble as 'ludicrous', while another finds Darbishire's 'lust for detail' completely overdone.

Needless to say, none of this does anything to dent the popularity of the houses, nor indeed the speed and vigour with which contemporary residents will leap to defend their unique and secluded little hamlet – as, for example, only a year or two ago, when a clear majority were up in arms about plans to extend one house with what the local *Camden Journal* described as a '*Teletubbies*-style sunken building with windows and light-wells cut into the lawns'.

Perhaps fortunately nothing came of that particular plan, and the future of Holly Village seems secure. There is nevertheless something slightly spooky about the place, not just in its self-conscious 'Stepford Wives' suburban perfection, but also in its close proximity to the eerily Gothic Highgate Cemetery. With several different architects working here at the same time and employing a very similar architectural style, the combined effect of cemetery and suburb is beautifully atmospheric, but these days slightly sinister.

PENTONVILLE PRISON
CALEDONIAN ROAD, N7

England's Own Death Row

After libelling the Prince Regent – somewhat unwisely referring to him as a 'fat Adonis' – the poet and essayist Leigh Hunt reportedly had a fairly comfortable time in his suite of cells at the progressive Horsemonger Lane Gaol. But in Pentonville, now London's oldest correctional facility, the regime was somewhat starker, despite it too being a so-called model prison based on Philadelphia's Eastern Penitentiary.

It took its name from one of the first new towns, a planned middle-class suburb laid out in the mid 1770s on the previously rural estate of Henry Penton MP, but which later became slum-ridden. When it was completed in 1842, the forbidding-looking gaol was nevertheless described in one account as 'extremely bright and cheerful and airy … a bit of a Crystal Palace stripped of all its contents'.

Unusually, its sponsors set out to reform the inmates rather than merely locking them up (or, as at Wormwood Scrubs thirty years later, requiring them to build their own cells). It was, even so, a hard place to do time. For one thing, the practice known as 'grinding the wind' had its origins at Pentonville, the invention of the crank having been made here. A hard-labour machine which remained in use until 1899, this required prisoners to push paddles through sand thereby achieving nothing beyond their physical exhaustion.

With each of them spending twenty-three hours a day in solitary confinement, the inmates must also have been bored stiff. To make things worse they wore hoods during their one-hour exercise period, the idea being that, if all they could see was their feet, they would have time and space to reflect on their crimes. For similar reasons, speech was completely forbidden and the warders were issued with felt overshoes in order to heighten the sepulchral feel of the place.

Little wonder, one might think, that upon their release so many inmates simply crossed the road and checked into the nearby Middlesex County Pauper Mental Asylum – in its day, Europe's largest.

But of course, in one sense these were the lucky ones, for many others never left at all and still lie beneath a well-kept lawn by the north-eastern wall. Surrounded by pretty flower beds and far from being an amenity for the other prisoners, this very particular little garden was to become the final resting place of all those who came here to be hanged: Crippen, Christie and 118 others executed sometime between 1902 (when Newgate was demolished and its gallows brought here) and 6 July 1961 when the practice was finally abolished and the condemned cell converted into a probation service staff room.

For much of this time the Home Office actually retained the services of two hangmen, one as 'No. 1' and the other as his assistant. But Pentonville remained pre-eminent, executing more prisoners in the twentieth century than any other British gaol. In fact, because by the 1930s so few other institutions even had their own gallows, the prison even operated a sort of takeaway service. Proximity to King's Cross and Euston made it the perfect choice, and for years what has since been described as a flat-pack execution kit could be sent by train to wherever it was needed.

NORTH-WEST LONDON

CAMDEN CATACOMBS
CHALK FARM ROAD, NW1

Pit Ponies in Central London

With secure employment for a couple of thousand years at least, it was nevertheless inevitable that horses would eventually give way to machines, and so it is interesting to find somewhere in the heart of London where the two once worked side by side.

The place in question lies between (or more correctly, beneath) the famous market at Camden Lock and the old bonded gin warehouse of W. & A. Gilbey. Extending under the Euston mainline and as far as the goods yard at Primrose Hill, it comprises a surprisingly extensive web of vaults and underground passageways, bearing witness to the area's former role as an important canal–railway interchange. As part of this, the network was constructed in the nineteenth century to provide stabling and tack space for the horses and pit ponies required at that time to shunt wagons around the yards above (also to and from the nearby Regent's or North Metropolitan Canal as it made its way from Paddington to the Thames at Limehouse).

Still owned by the inheritors of the British Rail property empire, but these days largely used for storage, the catacombs once provided subterranean entrances to the basements of several Victorian wharves and warehouses. Sadly, most are no longer easy to access, although their extent can be gauged by anyone walking above simply by plotting the many cast-iron grilles set into the road. Positioned at regular intervals in the road surface, these provided the working animals and their masters with a degree of natural light and ventilation.

Some further indication of the extent of the network can also be gleaned from the knowledge that the catacombs included their own underground canal basin, as well as a vast subterranean hall which once housed steam-powered winding gear employed to winch trains up the incline from Euston station. (When locomotive technology had progressed sufficiently to dispense with aids such as these stationary engines, the winding gear itself is said to have been sold on to the Russians.)

It is, however, still possible to glimpse a very small portion of the network during a visit to Camden's Stables Market, where many small retail units selling antiques, vintage clothing and other collectibles are housed in restored canalside buildings. These include some built into the Victorian brick arches of 1854, which run under the old North Western Railway Company sidings, and others in the listed Horse Hospital, which, as the name suggests, would once have been charged with caring for those animals injured pulling barges or shunting wagons.

REGENT'S CANAL
NW1 TO NW8

London's Forgotten Transport Network

A bit like an early watery version of the North Circular, but now one of the least known yet most delightful means of travelling across town, work began on the Regent's or North Metropolitan Canal in 1812, and it opened eight years later.

Thereafter, once joined with the Grand Union Canal (itself inaugurated in 1814 to provide a link between the Grand Junction

Canal and the Leicestershire and Northamptonshire Canals), the system grew rapidly, encompassing an extensive system of walk- and waterways, often surprisingly long tunnels and a number of other curious structures providing a useful through route from London and its docks all the way to Birmingham.

Today, however, especially where the narrow, calm waterways pass under the nose-to-tail traffic above, it feels like another world altogether – a parallel universe where one can get an unusual perspective on otherwise familiar corners of London, without encountering anybody but the odd angler or dog-walker along the way. It's true that progress this way is slow, but with no jams, traffic lights or hold-ups, one's average speed is probably no worse than if one were up above in a car, bus or taxi.

Certainly there is much to see, for the Regent's Canal alone passes under forty bridges and through a dozen locks. Elsewhere, most obviously in Little Venice, are some glorious houseboats, while the canal also provides the most unexpected view of London Zoo. Then there are the tunnels: Maida Vale, a comparative shorty at just 272yds, and beneath Islington another one of 960yds through which two traditional narrowboats can just about squeeze past each other.

Originally, of course, the boats would have been 'walked' through these tunnels, the crew lying on their backs on the roof of the vessel so they could walk along the arched bricks, while the tow-horses took a break and were led through the streets above. By 1826, however, Nash's long Islington Tunnel had acquired a steam tug and for more than a century this hauled itself and the narrowboats along a chain laid on the bed of the waterway.

Evidence of those working horses can still be seen on the giant iron pillars of Macclesfield Bridge, near the zoo. These have deep grooves worn in them by the tow-ropes – a not uncommon feature on old canalside bridges – although curiously these appear to be on the wrong side of the pillars.

The reason for this is because the bridge had to be completely rebuilt following a massive explosion in 1874 – an incident involving the fully laden barge *Tilbury* on its way from the Royal Gunpowder Mills at Waltham Abbey (see p. 216). Afterwards the decision was taken to erect the pillars the other way around in order to even up the wear. Perhaps unsurprisingly, given how little use is made of the canal, most Londoners, even those living in the borough, have never heard of Macclesfield Bridge, nor indeed its nickname: Blow-Up Bridge.

BULL AND BUSH
HAMPSTEAD WAY, NW3

London's Deepest Railway Station

Officially North End station – but more often known, if known at all, after the nearby pub made famous by a thousand cockney music-hall singalongs – in the end it probably doesn't matter what one calls it. This is because, while the rails, platforms and stairwells were all installed and working down the hill from Hampstead's Jack Straw's Castle, this particular station on the Northern Line was never officially opened nor used even once for its original purpose.

With the Northern Line set to take the record as the longest continuous railway tunnel in the world – the distance from East Finchley to Morden via Bank is some 17 miles, 528yds – it was built when there was a plan between the wars for the Hampstead Tube Company to extend the line even further.

Running both north and south of the existing line, it called for a new tunnel to be dug some 200ft beneath Hampstead Heath. Opposition to the proposal, unsurprisingly, was immediate, strong and vigorous. One objector even wrote to *The Times* propounding his theory that such a tunnel would act as a drain, effectively denying moisture to the vegetation on the Heath and flooding the line. The same writer was also concerned that the constant vibration would loosen tree-root systems thereby increasing the risk, supposing one such existed, of landslides into the residential parts of Hampstead.

In the end, the local population's articulate and well-organised 'Nimby' tendency met with some success, no doubt being helped by the scheduling of the Heath as a public open space, which removed the potential for large-scale housing development at this location and thus reduced the likely number of station users.

Consequently, while the line was continued through to Golders Green and beyond, what would have been the deepest station on the entire Underground network was quickly abandoned. Mothballed in 1906, it thus achieved the unique status of being the only one of London's more than forty so-called ghost stations to have been closed without ever having been used for its original purpose.

Fortunately, by the 1950s a new use had been found for it as London Transport's emergency headquarters in the event of a Cold War nuclear attack. Later still, it was used to house the control centre for a network of floodgates which were installed throughout the Underground. These could be lowered by remote control in order to seal off the tunnels in the event of an incursion from the Thames, but were themselves rendered redundant in 1985 when the Thames Barrier at Woolwich Reach became fully operational.

Thus, by 1993, its name had appeared on London Transport's prized list of disused Underground stations that were now available for rent. In contrast to the network's other ghosts, however, such as

Down Street, Dover Street and Brompton Road, there is no station-like structure on the surface and no maroon tiles; merely this anonymous white concrete blockhouse, no larger than a domestic tool shed, tucked away behind a conventional garden fence.

GOLDFINGER HOUSE
WILLOW ROAD, NW3

Putting Theory into Practice

An early and inspirational Modern Movement design, and unusual in that it is owned by the National Trust and therefore open to the public daily, Goldfinger House was designed by the architect best known for the looming Trellick Tower in North Kensington. Here in Hampstead he practised what he preached. Designing a home for himself and his family in 1939, he lived at 2 Willow Road until his death nearly fifty years later.

The architect in question was of course Erno Goldfinger, who was born in Budapest in 1902 but trained at the Ecole des Beaux Arts in Paris before, like so many of his fellow professionals and artists, being forced to flee the Nazis as they stampeded across Europe towards his native Hungary.

The three houses he built here (apparently to impress his in-laws) unfortunately required the demolition of some old cottages and this together with the sometimes uncompromising nature of his designs meant that he was never without his critics.

The local authority was one such, objecting to the houses before being overruled by the London County Council. Another was John Blackwell of Crosse & Blackwell, Goldfinger's cousin by marriage and a golfing buddy of James Bond creator Ian Fleming. As part of an ongoing spat with his relative, he persuaded Fleming to adopt the architect's name for his new villain. Fleming enjoyed the idea of settling scores in this way – in *The Man with the Golden Gun*, Scaramanga was named after an unpopular contemporary of the author's at Eton – and certainly there were a few interesting parallels between the fictional and real-life Goldfingers.

Both were Jewish émigrés who had come to Britain in the 1930s. Both reportedly had monstrous egos and, in the words of journalist Lewis Chester, both had 'an almost monomaniacal attachment to their own vision of the world which had its symbolism in a substance' – gold in one case, that is, and raw, undressed concrete in the other.

Needless to say, the non-fiction Goldfinger was not especially keen to be immortalised in this unflattering way and sought to prevent publication. In this he was, of course, unsuccessful and today as a result is somewhat overshadowed in the public imagination by his more famous, fictional counterpart.

Even so, describing him as having a 'monomaniacal attachment' to concrete seems a little too strong. It's true the Trellick Tower makes a somewhat brutal monument to the stuff, but his three connected houses in Willow Road are largely brick, relatively elegant, much sought after and, with their large picture windows, possessed of truly enviable views of the Heath.

The interior of No. 2, however, seems to have dated rather more than its exterior, in part perhaps because of its reliance on many materials which would have been considered 'advanced' for the day: items such as the linoleum tabletops, and the plywood, bent-steel and Bakelite fixtures and fittings, many of which were designed by Goldfinger himself. Even so, with pictures by the artist's wife, and other works by Henry Moore,

Max Ernst and Bridget Riley, the house now makes an intriguing period piece and is certainly far more interesting than a number of other twentieth-century properties acquired by the Trust.

CROCKER'S FOLLY
ABERDEEN PLACE, NW8

Entrepreneur's Dramatic Miscalculation

In any discussion of railway mania, one tends naturally to hear more about the successes than the failures, perhaps because the evidence for failure is rarely there to be seen in bricks and mortar. The building popularly known as Crocker's Folly is, however, London's one happy exception.

Forgotten, forlorn and, at the time of writing, sadly falling to pieces, this once vast Victorian gin palace – its scale and elaborate decoration wholly out of keeping with the residential environment in which it sits – was built by a late nineteenth-century speculator. Naming it the Crown Hotel, Frank Crocker was keen to serve the thousands of thirsty, hungry passengers arriving in the capital each day and alighting at the adjacent railway terminal.

The only trouble was, there was no adjacent railway terminal – nor, indeed, was there ever going to be one. Instead, as fast as Crocker's workmen beavered away to complete his precious investment, the navvies laying the rails for the Grand Central Railway pushed on past his pub and down the road to finish up at much more logical Marylebone.

Of course, with the benefit of hindsight, it seems highly unlikely that there were ever any serious plans to site the station

in this particular part of leafy St John's Wood. The street in question forms part of the once extensive Harrow School estate, and, like several others in the area, is named after one of the school governors, in this case former Foreign Secretary and Prime Minister George Hamilton-Gordon, Earl of Aberdeen (1784–1860).

The truth is that, while London as a whole may have welcomed the influence of the railway, most of the historic landlords and the well-heeled residents of this part of St John's Wood did not. Indeed, their opposition to the plan was so strong that the railway's backers were forced to spend such large sums of money answering their concerns that there was very little left of it by the time they reached Marylebone.

Thus, having spent a small fortune surveying and excavating a tunnel to take the line under the MCC's outfield at Lord's (to name just one example), they were actually forced to economise on their own stations. This is why Marylebone, the last of the great London main-line terminals to be built, is so modest in scale compared to, say, St Pancras or airy, spacious Liverpool Street.

That said, the efforts of the St John's Wood protesters were never going to be anything but partially successful, and by the turn of the century the railway had managed to acquire and destroy around 70 acres of the adjacent Eyre estate (which at nearly 200 acres is still, incredibly, owned by descendants of a follower of Richard the Lionheart). This in turn marked the beginning of the end for a once tranquil and charming residential area, one which had attracted artists, authors and philosophers including George Eliot, Landseer, Alma-Tadema and the naturalist T.H. Huxley to its green and pleasant streets and squares.

WEST LONDON

BROADCASTING HOUSE
PORTLAND PLACE, W1

What Gill Left Behind

From where nation shall speak unto nation – or moron unto moron, depending on your point of view and the time of day – the dazzling white Portland stone façade, bold art deco design and careful interpretation of Georgian proportions make Broadcasting House even now one of the most distinctive buildings in the capital. Indeed, despite being unfortunately sited, towering over the conical Bath stone spire of John Nash's All Souls' Church, it is also one of the best from the twentieth century.

The BBC's first proper home – until its completion in May 1932, Corporation staff were housed in a ramshackle collection of rooms on Savoy Hill – Broadcasting House has frequently been likened to a liner, although the intention of architect G. Val Myers was always to give London something to rival the extravagant style and scale of New York's thoroughly modern skyscrapers.

The site had previously been occupied by a house built by the architect James Wyatt for himself, from which many fireplaces and other internal features were removed to the Victoria and Albert Museum. Following its demolition in 1928 and the site's acquisition by the BBC, Myers was asked to provide twenty-two new studios, each of course to be effectively soundproofed both from the others and from the world outside. His solution was ingenious and he set about designing an inner core to house the studios, which would be surrounded by office and administration accommodation that would form a sort of protective outer shell.

In the event, the concept was not proved, however, and today broadcasters still complain about Tube trains trundling underneath and other extraneous noises. Nor did it take long for the BBC to outgrow its spacious new premises so more studios were soon commissioned in a disused roller-skating rink at Maida Vale, while in 1940 yet more staff were removed to Bush House, Aldwych.

That same year, the gleaming Broadcasting House was hastily painted battleship grey to make it less visible to enemy bombers, but on 15 October it was hit anyway. Seven people died and the world-famous gramophone library was completely destroyed. Nonetheless, brushing fallen plaster from his dinner jacket and soot off his script, Bruce Belfrage, down in the basement, continued reading the nine o'clock news with barely a pause for breath.

Today, the most exceptional features of the exterior are still the carvings by Eric Gill over the main entrance. The BBC reportedly wanted these figures to represent Ariel and Prospero from Shakespeare's *Tempest*, the former, being a spirit of the air, somehow symbolising the future of broadcasting. But Gill always claimed that he saw the figures as representing God and Man, also insisting he be allowed to work on them *in situ* while wearing a monk's habit with nothing on underneath – and never mind the female staff entering the building down below.

Later it was also discovered that Gill had cheekily found time to carve a relief of a girl's face on Prospero's backside, and to render Ariel suspiciously well endowed.

BURLINGTON ARCADE
PICCADILLY, W1

Walk, Don't Run

The archetype and best known of a handful of private shopping arcades which survive in this part of the West End, much of the fame of Burlington Arcade relies not so much on its apparent exclusivity as on its uniquely strange by-laws. Enforced as always by a traditionally clad, top-hatted beadle, these regulations forbid pedestrians entering the elegant Regency precinct to run, whistle or open an umbrella – although fortunately these days visitors are permitted to carry their own bags.

The development's origins date back to 1818 when Lord George Cavendish commissioned his architect Samuel Ware to design a covered shopping arcade of the sort then popular in France. When asked, his lordship insisted it was purely 'for the sale of jewellery and fancy articles of fashionable demand, for the gratification of the publick and to give employment to industrious females'. But unofficially it was said by his detractors that his desire was merely to prevent passers-by throwing oyster shells and other unpleasant rubbish over the wall and into the courtyard and gardens of Burlington House, for which Cavendish had recently paid £70,000.

Whatever the reason, when it opened the following year his elegant arcade was an immediate success. By this time, of course, the more fashionable shops were already moving out of the old City, the shrewder retailers choosing to follow their clientele as the epicentre of smart London moved inexorably westwards. For these customers such developments (as indeed they still do) offered a welcome retreat from the swirling bustle and noise of London's major streets. Then, unlike now, they also provided somewhere for the better class of prostitute to display herself, before at a given signal she disappeared into one shop or another and to an upstairs room suitably arranged.

In 1911, and absolutely not with this particular trade in mind, an additional storey was added to the arcade. The architect this time was E. Beresford Pite who took the opportunity to renew the Piccadilly entrance while attaching the arms of its then owner, Lord Chesham (hence the beadles being traditionally recruited from the 10th Hussars, Chesham's old regiment).

As it happened, Professor Pite was back again twenty years later, by which time ownership had passed from Chesham to the Prudential Assurance Company. This time he redesigned the south entrance and, to the horror of the *Architectural Review*, ruined his own masterpiece by giving 'full scope to the mahogany shopfitting "expert" [so that] the whole appearance of the Arcade is spoiled'.

With no immediate point of comparison, it is hard to know whether most visitors today would concur with that view or even care. Instead, with its much-copied glass roof, carefully and minutely detailed little shopfronts, and above all those lavish displays behind the glass of desirable if in the main wholly impractical goods, Burlington Arcade and its pretty Piccadilly rival remain, after nearly 200 years, as fashionable as ever.

CAFÉ DE PARIS
COVENTRY STREET, W1

Thrilling the Three Thousand

A dance hall in the 1950s, later becoming a disco and more recently a popular venue for so-called speed-dating, back in 1924 the basement of the Rialto Cinema was home to the famous Café de Paris and as such was one of the most celebrated addresses in town for the next two decades.

Not that Coventry Street itself was ever anything special, and nor is it now. Named after Henry Coventry, Charles II's Secretary of State from 1672 to 1679, it was completed in 1681 but almost immediately acquired a reputation for dissipation and disreputable behaviour. This reputation proved an enduring one too, the antiquarian J.T. Smith finding in 1846 'a number of gaming-houses in the neighbourhood at the present time, so that the bad character of the place is at least two centuries old, or ever since it was built upon'.

The opening of the Café coincided with the new craze for cocktails – 'the most reprehensible form of alcoholic abuse', according to the medical authorities of the day – and it rapidly became the pre-eminent nightclub of its age. In this it was helped by the friendship of its Danish owner, Martin Poulsen, with the Prince of Wales, HRH dropping in several times a month. The club's popularity was thus more or less assured – not just among celebrities either, but crucially among the 'Upper Three Thousand' as well, this being the numerical extent of the liveliest, most social members of the Establishment.

Later, with Princess Margaret and the Duchess of Kent in the audience, Noel Coward made his cabaret debut in the club's oval-shaped main room which was said to have been modelled on the ballroom of the *Lusitania*. David Niven met his future wife here and Marlene Dietrich came for six weeks; also Charlie Chaplin and Cole Porter, who gave the first public performance of 'Miss Otis Regrets'. Various members of the Churchill and Kennedy clans were also spotted here from time to time.

Add royal patronage to the mix – not just Edward and Mrs Simpson, but also the future George VI and his Queen, and our own Queen Elizabeth II who had her coming-out party on the premises – and the place seemed unassailable. Indeed even the war wasn't going to be allowed to spoil the party, and at the outbreak of hostilities an order was placed for 25,000 bottles of champagne, oysters and caviar, the owner pulling in the punters with his talk of it being 'twenty feet underground' and so the safest club in London.

Alas, Martin Poulsen spoke too soon and in 1941, at 9.50 on the evening of 8 March, a German bomb hit the building above. The premises were wrecked, in the process killing the bandleader 'Snakehips' Johnson, more than eighty revellers and indeed Poulsen himself.

Eventually the club reopened (in July 1944) but now as a venue for entertaining the troops. The Dagenham Girl Pipers replaced Dietrich and the duchesses, and with 'other ranks' now packing out the stalls, 675 cases of champagne which had somehow survived the bomb were taken away and auctioned off. For the Café de Paris, the good times were clearly over.

SHEPHERD MARKET
CURZON STREET, W1

Built to Banish the Hullabaloo

Built in 1735–46 on the site of the old May Fair to serve the large aristocratic houses on Piccadilly, architect and developer Edward Shepherd's little precinct of shops and taverns still retains its small-scale, domestic, eighteenth-century feel – even though the aristocrats are mostly long gone, along with the servants who would once have thronged these passageways on their way to get the weekly provisions.

Once London would have had several such places, many built expressly to serve the clusters of first-quality houses being thrown up by developers as they pushed the boundaries of London further and further from its historic centre. By 1700, for example, St James's Market had a paved alleyway connecting it via Charles II Street to the ducal houses of Henry Jermyn's St James's Square. (Thus enabling what Robert Seymour described in his 1735 *Survey of the Cities of London and Westminster* as 'country butchers, higglers and the like' to sell goods – apparently at a handsome 25 per cent premium – to 'Stewards of the People of Quality, who spare no price to furnish their Lord's Houses with what is nice and delicate'.)

Sadly, this and most others have now gone or been so altered over the years as to leave Shepherd Market alone as a reminder of the amenities which would been drawn to the stable yards and kitchens of London's best addresses. It's a unique reminder, too, of how adept the Georgians were when it came to attractive but practical town planning.

Active in many parts of Mayfair and St James's – for example at the beautifully preserved corner house at 4 St James's Square – Shepherd was himself certainly well placed to know what such houses required in terms of shops and services. He was also shrewd enough to realise that even though the historic but riotous and disorderly May Fair had been suppressed, probably the only way to stop undesirables congregating here was to build over the land.

For that reason alone. the residents of the surrounding streets and squares must have breathed a sigh of relief when he commenced the construction of his new market house. A two-storey structure with shops below and an informal theatre in the great room in the space above, at the very least it reduced by one the available venues for what one contemporary commentator described as 'drunkenness, fornication, gaming and lewdness'.

Since then there has naturally been much redevelopment. Nonetheless, and while many buildings have mid-nineteenth-century dates on them, the atmosphere is still very much of the eighteenth, suggesting careful refurbishment rather than wholesale rebuilding.

As a result, especially if the tightly drawn grid of narrow streets and alleyways is entered via this covered passageway off Curzon Street, the impression is still very much that of a small village. An expensive village, as its address suggests, but one which is nevertheless surprisingly unprecious, so that today, in the summer at lunchtime or as somewhere to meet for an early evening drink, Shepherd Market really does take some beating.

TYBURN CONVENT
HYDE PARK PLACE, W2

Unexpected Haven of Tranquillity

Taking its name from the *teoburna* or 'boundary stream' which flows from Shepherd's Well in Hampstead to the Thames at Pimlico, Tyburn Convent was founded only in 1902 but is a shrine to the ancient Tyburn martyrs who were executed on this site – home to the famous 'Tyburn Tree' – during the Protestant Reformation.

The 105 martyrs were among the estimated 50,000 individuals hanged here between 1196 and 1783. The first was the Prior of the London Charterhouse, John Houghton, in 1535, the last the Primate of All Ireland a century and a half later. Both died on a triangular gallows large enough to dispatch twenty-one at a time.

Public executions were traditionally official public holidays. Often followed by grisly drawing and quartering, which is why so many butchers were recruited as executioners, the idea was that seeing a man brought here to die (and enjoying his last drink at the entrance to St-Giles-in-the-Fields' churchyard) would act as a deterrent. In fact they proved just the opposite and quickly became occasions for public drunkenness and rowdiness as well as providing the perfect opportunity for pick-pockets and prostitutes of the town to go about their business. Accordingly, in 1783 the gallows were removed to Newgate – Defoe's 'emblem of hell', a place Casanova described on leaving as 'an abode of misery and despair' – and in 1868 the executions were finally brought 'in house'.

By this time too, the position of Roman Catholics in Britain was improving and moves were afoot to build a shrine to the martyrs on the spot where so many of them had met their end. To this end a house was acquired in Hyde Park Place and in 1902 given over to an order of Benedictine nuns called the Sisters of the Adoration of the Sacred Heart of Jesus of Montmartre.

Twenty-five of the sisters now live behind the locked doors fronting on to the busy Bayswater Road. An enclosed order, meaning they never leave the cloistered community unless they are sick or dying, they inhabit three linked buildings on the site which house the nuns' cells, a simple, white-walled chapel, a library, kitchen, refectory and chapter house, all surrounded by a peaceful, high-walled garden.

Underneath there is now a crypt containing bones and other relics of the martyrs, for whose souls the nuns – traditionally dressed in a black veil, white guimpe around the neck, a full-length habit and a white cowl during services – pray seven times each day. The public can join them for Mass, but remain seated behind a grille.

With no apostolic role requiring (or indeed allowing) the nuns to leave the convent to carry out charity work or teaching, they spend their days praying and studying, with just one hour a day to relax in the gardens, or play snooker or Scrabble, and just ninety minutes a month for visits from friends and family.

In 1989, however, the order paid host to the Nuns' World Snooker Championship, raising around £50,000 for the renovation of its buildings in an event which has now become an annual fixture. 'Playing snooker,' says Vatican Archbishop Luigi Barbarito, 'gives you firm hands and helps to build up character.' It is, he insists, the ideal recreation for a dedicated nun.

CHISWICK HOUSE
BURLINGTON LANE, W4

Perfect Renaissance Recreation

In its correct, pure form the Palladian villa of the Italian Renaissance was never well suited to the English climate or our way of life; nor for that matter were creations such as Andrea Palladio's famous Villa Rotonda ever really an entirely practical proposition back home in Vicenza.

It is therefore hardly surprising that relatively few here have attempted close copies. Unsurprising too that the houses built by the few who have been tempted – such as Colen Campbell's Mereworth Castle in Kent (1723), and Henbury Hall in Cheshire, created by Felix Kelly and Julian Bicknell in the mid 1980s – still appear so singular and exotic when placed in an English setting.

In fact, barely a handful of such houses were ever built in the British Isles and of these even the best known, the third Earl of Burlington's iconic country house at Chiswick, was never really intended as a residence. Instead its creator stayed next door in his Jacobean mansion, using the building we see today merely as somewhere to display his sculptures and paintings, to house his library and to entertain his wide circle of artistic friends.

Completed in 1729, with the Earl's famous protégé William Kent creating some spectacular interiors under the influence of Inigo Jones, its aesthetically correct but quite impractical design was perhaps best described by Lord Hervey who characterised the finished house as 'too small to inhabit, and too large to hang on one's watch'. The style was nevertheless hugely influential, as indeed were the gardens which surrounded it.

Also laid out by Kent (here working with Charles Bridgman), these were the first in England to abandon the stiff, more formal Dutch style. Instead, the two men adopted a more naturalistic approach with a variety of follies located in strategic positions around the landscape to complement the design of the house. Some of these can still be seen today, including a Doric column and an Ionic temple, various obelisks, a genuine Inigo Jones gateway (brought from Beaufort House in Chelsea) and Roman statuary originally arranged around the Emperor Hadrian's villa at Tivoli.

The Burlington line having reached its conclusion in 1753 – despite quantities of asses' milk and the use of a bespoke 'machine chair' specially ordered from London, the third Earl died here of palsy on 3 December – the house and grounds were inherited by the fourth Duke of Devonshire. His heir felt compelled to extend the carefully considered house, commissioning James Wyatt to build matching but somewhat inappropriate wings to the north and south, and eventually it became a private mental home when the eighth duke removed to Chatsworth.

Probably fortunately, the house then came into public ownership, being acquired by Middlesex County Council in 1928 and expertly restored by the Ministry of Works. Burlington's Jacobean mansion had mostly disappeared by this time and in 1952 Wyatt's wings were also removed, thereby restoring the house to its creator's original design. No less significantly, these removals also left it standing in relative and splendid isolation, much as Palladio's prototype had done 1,000 miles away and 450 years before.

KENSAL GREEN CEMETERY
HARROW ROAD, W10

The New Fashion for Funerals

With space having long ago run out in the historic burial grounds and churchyards of the inner city (there were widespread reports of old coffins being dug up to make way for new ones, and bodies being so inadequately buried that they were easy prey for grave robbers), in 1830 Parliament finally acknowledged the need for graveyards to be removed 'to places where they would be less prejudicial to the health of the inhabitants'.

Accordingly, that same year Kensal Green became the first of the great commercial cemeteries in the metropolis (which today extend to more than 3,000 acres). Then, as now, it was run under the auspices of the General Cemetery Company, which planted hundreds of trees on 54 acres acquired for the purpose before commissioning a vast Doric arch by way of an entrance, a Greek Revival chapel for conventional funerals and an Ionic one for non-conformists at its eastern extremity.

With considerable publicity and every mod con, including a hydraulic lift linking the main chapel to the catacombs below, the enterprise proved to be an immediate success. In less than a decade, GCC's share price had more than doubled to £52; with the burials here of Princess Sophia and, in a gigantic granite tomb opposite the main chapel, of Augustus, Duke of Sussex (both children of George III), the fashion for these so-called gardens of the deceased was soon well established.

Part of their appeal was clearly aesthetic, and with its colonnades and catacombs, the gravel paths and extensive

plantings, Kensal Green very much set the pace. Certainly G.K. Chesterton thought so – in 'The Rolling English Road' he wrote of it: 'There is good news yet to hear and fine things to be seen, before we go to Paradise by way of Kensal Green' – and the celebrated landscape gardener J.C. Loudon chose to be buried here in 1843.

Before long, many more of the great and good were buying up plots here too, including the writers Thackeray, Trollope and Wilkie Collins, the poet Thomas Hood, the Revd Sydney Smith and Byron's celebrated publisher, John Murray. In 1849, Sir Marc Isambard Brunel, followed by his wife Sophia and (ten years later) their son Isambard Kingdom, were buried here, as well as the great showman Blondin after his death at Niagara House, Ealing.

These days the most celebrated incumbent, however, must be General James M. Barry. He died in 1865, presumably reasonably confident that history would show this one-time senior inspector of the Army Medical Department to have been a fine soldier and a really first-class medical and military administrator.

When it came to his embalming, however, it was discovered that Barry was actually a woman, and that the 'M' really stood for Miranda. Despite being described by acquaintances as 'the most wayward of men' and 'beardless' in appearance, none had succeeded in guessing the truth. Instead, concealing her gender all her life, Miranda Barry had managed to rise to the very peak of her profession; indeed, only posthumously has this formidable individual been recognised as the country's first qualified female doctor – as well, of course, as the Army's first female general.

MELBURY ROAD
WEST KENSINGTON, W14

Artists' Olympus

A creative enclave of quite a different kind to the aforementioned Shoreditch Triangle, west London's famous nineteenth-century artists' colony comprises some fine and distinctive houses, plus many famous incumbents including G.F. Watts – a friend of Lord Holland's, and the first to arrive – Luke Fildes, Holman Hunt and Marcus Stone, William Burges and the sculptor Sir William Hamo Thorneycroft.

Originally part of the Holland House Estate – which in 1859 came into the possession of the splendidly named Henry Fox-Strangways, Baron Strangways of Woodford Strangways and fifth Earl of Ilchester – the road was laid out in 1875 and derived its name from the family estate in Dorset.

Inevitably, with so many of the vast detached houses being designed by the leading names of the day, it was never going to be anything but grand. Not that this stopped Frederick, Lord Leighton, who lived around the corner, from insisting, somewhat disingenuously, that he and the other artists residing hereabouts actually lived in 'a mews'.

Such a notion is quickly dealt with by even the briefest glance up the street. Designed by Richard Norman Shaw, Halsey Ricardo and indeed Burges himself, and mostly built during the closing decades of the nineteenth century, these houses more than anything underline the fact that both financially and socially artists were never held in higher esteem than at this time.

Able at last to move in the most fashionable circles, the houses the new aesthetic elite chose to build and occupy were clearly intended to demonstrate by their size and style that these men were something special.

Burges, for example, built Tower House at No. 29 for himself and (designed as 'a model house of the fifteenth century') it has plenty to say about his preoccupations at the time. Dominated by this immense round tower with a conical roof looking like something straight out of the pages of *Rapunzel* or *Sleeping Beauty*, it is similar in style to Cardiff Castle and Castell Coch, on which he worked with the third Marquess of Bute. Its most remarkable room, though, is probably his own bedroom, designed in such a way that, when lying in a haze of laudanum, Burges could imagine himself to be lying at the bottom of the sea.

Somewhat more sober are Nos 2 and 4, built for Hamo Thorneycroft – one to live in, another to let – while No. 8 was built by Norman Shaw for Marcus Stone. Designed in Norman Shaw's highly fashionable Queen Anne style, its distinctive tall windows were to light the painter's studio. (The same architect was also responsible for Luke Fildes' house at No. 31, but this has been substantially altered over the years.)

Another plot of land was acquired by a railwayman rather than an artist, Sir Alexander Rendel, who, as one might perhaps expect of a great engineer, commissioned Halsey Ricardo with his interest in novel and advanced materials. The result was a pair of semi-detached houses, now at Nos 55 and 57, on which work began in 1894. While they lack the fanfare and flourish of Ricardo's extraordinary Debenham House in nearby Addison Road, their façade of ox-blood glazed bricks certainly makes them stand out.

SOUTH-WEST LONDON

BLUE BALL YARD
ST JAMES'S STREET, SW1

No Mere Mews

A rare and largely unspoilt mid-eighteenth-century stableyard surviving in the heart of the West End, Blue Ball Yard is approached through an archway off the west side of St James's Street, the restricted, slightly anonymous entrance giving unexpectedly on to a wide, well-preserved and highly picturesque cobbled yard.

In approximately this form it has been here since at least 1680, although the coach houses later used as garaging date from only 1741–42 when it would have provided servants' accommodation for the grand houses clustering around St James's Palace, as well as somewhere for the aristocrats to stable their horses and park their carriages. Accordingly, at that time it was known simply as Stable Yard, the name being changed a few years later to commemorate the Blue Ball Tavern which stood in the adjacent street until it was demolished in 1754.

Naturally the reliance on horsepower meant there were once many more such yards in this area, including what is now Little St James's Street (which provided stabling as early as 1651) and Pickering Place, which dates from around 1690 when it was known as Stroud's Court and is described on p. 132. Many more can be seen on Richard Horwood's map of 1792–99, but unfortunately these have since been modified beyond recognition or wiped out by large-scale development.

Blue Ball Yard, however, has prospered, its attractive foliage and well-kept air having much to do with its proximity to the

luxurious Stafford Hotel in nearby St James's Place. Taking over part of the yard, formerly an antiquarian bookseller and later a fine-art picture framers, the privately owned hotel has created within the historic shell what it calls the Carriage House. This comprises a series of luxurious suites, each named after an illustrious racehorse, and was officially 'opened' by one of them: Seagram, winner of the 1991 Grand National.

Some things have not changed so much, though, so that for example after nearly 250 years the split entrance to the yard – with an opening for vehicles and another, narrower one for pedestrians – still hints at the original ownership of the yard. Unusually this was shared between two separate freeholders, the wall dividing the two modern entrances marking the boundary between that portion of the yard owned by Thomas Freke and the southern portion which was held by Charles Godolphin. It seems likely that the yard we see today was formed jointly by these two men.

BRIDGEWATER HOUSE
CLEVELAND ROW, SW1

Canals to Shipping

Northumberland House was removed from Trafalgar Square in 1874, Devonshire House on Piccadilly was demolished in the 1920s and Norfolk House disappeared from St James's Square in 1938. All in all, the fate of London's grand ducal mansions has not been a happy one, which makes the almost total anonymity of this rare survivor even more of a mystery.

It's true of course that the Bridgewater dukedom has not survived either, but then when it comes to distinctive extinctions dukes seem always to fare less well than other ranks, with only twenty-four titles surviving of the 162 so far granted. In fact, the Bridgewater dynasty lasted for a mere two generations, the third and last duke dying in 1803 barely half a century after the first.

But against this one has to consider the house itself: huge, architecturally magnificent and surprisingly little known, despite the immediate proximity of Lancaster House and St James's Palace, it manages to completely dominate this quiet corner of the West End. And it does so even though most people passing by its immense façade clearly have little or no idea about what it is.

In fact, while indisputably ducal, its appearance today depends not so much on the dukes but on the last one's great nephew and eventual heir. Utilising the vast fortune amassed by his canal-building forebear – the so-called father of inland navigation – in 1840 Sir Francis Leveson Gower (later created the Earl of Ellesmere) had Charles Barry rebuild the dukes' original house in a grand Italianate style in order to better accommodate his vast and quite remarkable collection of more than 300 paintings.

Even more remarkable was the fact that his family allowed the public in to view this collection – this at a time when, unlike country houses, those in town were almost never open to visitors – which must have been made a good deal easier by the positively museum-like scale of Barry's stupendous design.

Occupying a massive, almost square plot of more than 20,000 square feet, it is indeed as large as many corporate or public buildings. The main picture gallery, for example, occupies almost the whole of the north range and dwarfs many public galleries, being sufficiently large that in 1928 the Ellesmeres were able to host a ball here for a staggering 1,500 guests, in addition to what Lady Ellesmere later referred to as 'several hundred' gate-crashes.

Little wonder then that, with its principal façade a full 165ft in width, it is today one of London's most palatial and most imposing private homes. And, incredibly, it is still a private home: having been sold by the Ellesmeres to an insurance company which let it to British Oxygen in the 1950s, it was snapped up for a reported £19 million in 1981 by another water-based billionaire, Greek shipping and banking magnate John Latsis, to use as his London residence.

CHELSEA COLLEGE OF ART & DESIGN
ATTERBURY STREET, SW1

A New Piazza Revealed

Almost as fortunate as the students and staff of Greenwich University, who were able to take over the sensational group of riverside buildings comprising the Old Royal Naval College (see p. 179), the administrative reshuffle of five art and fashion colleges to create a new University of the Arts London saw one component – the Chelsea College of Art & Design – moving into these former Royal Army Medical College premises on Millbank in 2005.

Handily placed for Tate Britain next door, but until that date little known and (or obvious reasons) rarely open to the public, the military establishment had its origins in the new Army Medical School established at Fort Pitt, Chatham, in 1860. It moved up from Kent only in 1907, into this range of pleasant neo-Georgian buildings designed for it by Woodd & Ainslie.

Attached by a raised corridor to the RAMC Officers' HQ Mess next door, for the best part of a century the college provided its students with specialised postgraduate teaching in a range of military and medical disciplines, as well as a secure home for the Barry Room and the VC Room.

The first of these takes its name not from the famous architect but from General James M. Barry, the aforementioned surgeon who was discovered to be a woman after his death. The second, rather more significantly, was named in memory of no fewer than twenty-seven medical Victoria Cross holders: the Royal Army Medical Corps enjoying the not inconsiderable distinction of being the third most successful army unit in this regard. Beaten into third place by the Royal Artillery and the Royal Engineers, what is perhaps even more remarkable is that two of those RAMC recipients were awarded the decoration twice, an achievement shared by only one other individual in the medal's more than 150-year history.

Of the three, Lieutenant Colonel Arthur Martin-Leake (1874–1953) is unique in that his valour was recognised in two different wars. He received his first VC in the Boer War, a bar being added to this in the First World War, for which he volunteered, being clearly too old to be conscripted. The second, Captain Noel Godfrey Chavasse (1884–1917), meanwhile died of wounds sustained at Ypres, coincidentally after being transported by the 46th Field Ambulance, Martin-Leake's own unit. Even more extraordinary is the fact that the third double-VC, Captain Charles Upham – with no RAMC connection, he died in 1994 aged 86 – was actually related by marriage to Captain Chavasse.

Interestingly, the Mess having been built over the site of the old Millbank Penitentiary, a feature always pointed out to visitors is the series of bollards in the central courtyard. In the days when the vast penitentiary still dominated this reach of the river – shaped like a six-pointed star, it covered an incredible 7 acres – these were used to moor the barges which brought the prisoners awaiting transportation to Australia. One bollard, indeed, is said to have marked the position of a tunnel under the road through which these unfortunates would pass, hence the phrase 'Down Under'.

CROWN PASSAGE
PALL MALL, SW1

Where Cavaliers Still Congregate

Even if one accepts the description of London as a collection of separate but connected villages, one is still surprised and delighted to come across such a crowded and positively Dickensian little alleyway as this one running off the St James's Palace end of Pall Mall.

Dark but lively, a real discovery if you can actually find it (look out for the blue and white flag jutting out from Quebec House), it differs from the majority of London's similarly old and narrow byways because, while many of those have become dank hangouts for the homeless – or, worse still, informal stopping-off places for drunks caught short – Crown Passage

still buzzes with activity thanks to a cheerful jumble of odd shops, bustling cafés and, of course, an historic pub.

The latter – 'London's last village pub' – is actually one of two Red Lions in St James's, the other being a quite outstanding little Victorian gin palace in Duke of York Street. That one's a fine example of the nineteenth-century taste for over-decoration: lush and plush, with elaborate carved and deeply polished mahogany everywhere, etched-glass panels and gleaming cut-glass mirrors, and a genuine 'Lincrusta' or embossed decorated paper ceiling.

This one, though, like Crown Passage itself, is Georgian and altogether far simpler. Certainly, its black timber frontage and leaded lights suggest an even earlier pub on the same site, as do the sturdy brackets for gas lighting, although electric lights have now been substituted. In fact, the Red Lion claims to have the second-oldest licence in the West End and has unquestionably been owned by the same brewery for at least two centuries.

It is also where, on the last weekend in January, cavaliers in full rig crowd in to lament the death of their beloved monarch, executed in nearby Whitehall on 30 January 1649. None, however, has so far been able to confirm the rumoured existence of a secret tunnel through to St James's Palace, apparently excavated for Charles II and Nell Gwynne. Mind you, as she too had a house opposite, one wonders why they would have arranged to meet in a pub.

Nevertheless, the real charm of Crown Passage is that, even now, there is more here than just memories and an old pub. Instead it continues to provide services of real value to those lucky enough to live in this most coveted corner of the West End. Thus, after walking its length and emerging into King Street, one can well believe the claim that it is still possible, without leaving the passage, to hire a chimney sweep, be measured for a suit or have a hat made, buy your week's groceries and a daily paper, have your hair cut and arrange for your dry cleaning to be done while you nip into the pub or a café for a quick one. Indeed, one suspects that even the more august tradesmen in nearby Jermyn Street, with all their royal warrants and precious pedigrees, would have quite a job to match all that.

NAZI MEMORIAL
CARLTON HOUSE TERRACE, SW1

Dark Days and Dog Days

A Nazi memorial in London would be strange enough, even were it not situated right at the heart of England's old imperial quarter. Nevertheless, here it is, just yards from Wellington's personal mounting blocks, in the shadow of the great column raised to the memory of the Grand Old Duke of York, and hard by memorials to Edward VII, 'Scott of the Antarctic' and Sir John Franklin. A carefully tended Nazi grave – and what's more it belongs to a dog.

Described on the stone as *Eine treuer begleiter* ('a true companion'), the canine in question is an Alsatian named Giro. He died apparently after making an unwise connection with some exposed electrical wiring and was buried here in February 1934 while his master – Dr Leopold G.A. von Hoesch (1881–1936) – was serving his country as the German ambassador to the Court of St James's.

At this time, of course, relations between Britain and Germany were cool, certainly, but more wary than openly warlike. Even so, it is curious to think that, while the façades of Nash's Carlton House Terrace and indeed several more significant memorials in this area were to suffer considerable bomb damage at the hands of Germans by the end of the decade, Giro's grave managed to remain untouched and undamaged. Situated under a tree at the top of the steps between the former embassy and the Institute of Contemporary Arts, a glass case has more recently been built around it to ensure it stays that way.

Von Hoesch himself died of a stroke two years after the dog and, in accordance with the diplomatic practices then current, was given a momentous send-off. This included several British cabinet members leading the mourners, a nineteen-gun salute in nearby St James's Park and a detachment of Grenadier Guards to accompany the ceremonial gun carriage on which his body was borne to Victoria station.

After the ceremonials, he was replaced by the reviled Joachim von Ribbentrop, who quickly caused a minor scandal by greeting King George VI with a straight-arm salute.

In pretty short order he also expanded his country's embassy by having 8 and 9 Carlton House Terrace knocked through into a single building. In fact, he had originally hoped to plant an example of the Third Reich's brand of brutalist architecture right in the centre of the British capital, almost certainly something designed by the Führer's favourite architect and fellow Nazi, Albert Speer. But in the event, he settled for something more modest, having the interior remodelled by his wife – with the centrepiece an immense staircase made of marble said to have been contributed to the project by Benito Mussolini.

Since 1967, however, the building has housed the Royal Society and while rumours abound of various swastikas hidden beneath carpets, the interior today appears reassuringly free of Nazi iconography.

NELSON'S COLUMN
TRAFALGAR SQUARE, SW1

Slow to Acknowledge a True Hero

The heart of Empire, and so famous as to be almost unknown, most who come to Trafalgar Square do so only because they feel they ought to and few, one suspects, ever pause long enough to explore the place properly or realise what a hard time it had coming into being.

Take the famous centrepiece, for example, which at 145ft is still the world's tallest Corinthian column. William Railton won £200 for his design when it was chosen from more than 160 different drawings, plans and models submitted as part of a well-publicised competition – but for him and for everyone else involved it was a struggle all the way.

Railton's design, for example, was selected only after a second competition as the first produced such a poor crop of entries that none was considered suitable. Examples included a gigantic pyramid, an octagonal Gothic cenotaph, a statue not of Nelson but of William IV (the 'Sailor King'), others of mermaids apparently playing water polo, even an immense globe supported on the figures of Fame, Victory, Neptune and Britannia. There was one other column, but creator James Hakewill put Nelson at its base (as if standing before the mast) insisting that it was inappropriate for a 'mere subject, however heroic, to look down on Royalty'.

Precisely this kind of delay and dithering was to dog the entire project. Typical of the confusion – this was all taking place more than thirty-five years after Nelson's actual demise, and even then, Landseer's lions were to take another quarter of a century to arrive – it wasn't even the eventual winner who got to carve Nelson's likeness, but the runner-up. Not that many these days remember the name of Edmund Baily who did it, or indeed that of Railton, whose column most of the public at the time clearly didn't like.

Baily was also forced to modify his plans when no shipper could be found to transport the massive piece of stone for the statue. This had been obtained 'without profit' from a quarry owned by the Duke of Buccleuch, but in the event it broke in two during its removal, thereby solving the problem. The issue of the funding was equally shambolic, the money being raised by public subscription but surprisingly slowly given Nelson's popularity and the almost mythic status he had acquired at his death.

This may have been because the original intention to also commemorate the 3,827 officers, seamen and marines who had been killed or wounded alongside him had been lost. Eventually the money came in, though, albeit long after the work had been completed, with the Queen contributing the most (£500) and a Mrs Beeby the least, at 2s 6d.

Nor was poor old Nelson accorded much more respect once he was finally in place. In 1888, for example, he was hit by lightning and his remaining (left) arm broken. A temporary repair was made using metal 'bandages' at the time, but not until 2006 was the job finally done properly. Then, behind the elaborate scaffold and shrouding shown here, Nelson finally received the proper medical attention due an authentic hero.

PICKERING PLACE
ST JAMES'S STREET, SW1

London's Smallest Square

Pickering Place is a tiny, irregularly shaped, paved square, thought to be the smallest such public open space in London. A gas-lit courtyard, which until 1812 was known as Pickering Court, it is reached through a narrow eighteenth-century oak-panelled tunnel and is perhaps most famous for being the place in which was fought the last public duel in England.

Proving this, mind you, seems an impossibility, but certainly given its location in the heart of clubland (and its very real seclusion), it is an appealing and plausible notion that, when duelling was routine, two fiery young blades may have slipped out – of White's, or the Cocoa Tree, the Thatched House or one of several nameless gambling dens in the area – and into this small, concealed space to settle a personal score.

More certain, though at first glance no easier to credit, is that from 1842 this little enclave was also home to the official Legation from the Republic of Texas to the Court of St James's. In fact, a plaque on the panelled wall attests to this, having been erected by the Anglo-Texan Society to mark Texas joining the Union in 1845, some ten years after securing its independence from Mexico.

The four tall but quite modest houses on the narrow, stone-flagged courtyard were built in 1731 by James Pickering, son-in-law of the Widow Bourne whose grocery store was to evolve into the eighth-generation family-run wine merchants which still thrives next door. He built the individual houses over his own garden and workshop, and today Berry Brothers and Rudd's famously spacious cellars, a cool and temperature-controlled home to more than 200,000 bottles of rare ports and other vintages, run under the courtyard and down to Pall Mall.

The contrast is striking between the self-confident grandeur of Pall Mall and St James's Square, and the more laid-back, rather raffish feel of Pickering Place (where for some years Graham Greene kept a set of rooms overlooking the courtyard). Striking, that is, but happily not uncharacteristic of this historic corner of the West End. Indeed, despite the clearly astronomical values of its ancient freeholds (and the fact that, with nearly sixty listed Grade I and Grade II buildings, and perhaps a hundred more listed Grade II, it has the highest concentration of such buildings in the country), St James's as a whole seems somehow able to cling on to its little eccentricities and charms.

PORTSMOUTH SHUTTER TELEGRAPH LINE
HORSE GUARDS, SW1

Early Information Superhighway

In the eighteenth century, carrying an important dispatch from the Admiralty in Whitehall to the naval base at Portsmouth, good men riding hard were said to have taken more than four and a half hours to deliver a single message. Clearly a more efficient means of communication was badly needed, and in 1795 the Royal Navy set out to devise one by means of an optical telegraph system linking Whitehall and the coast with a chain of signalling stations. Initially a shutter system was used and what became known as the Portsmouth Shutter Telegraph Line soon comprised ten stations going south, with another twenty-two being added in 1806 to deliver messages 200 miles south-west to Plymouth.

In London, starting out at the Admiralty, the necessary signalling equipment was located at Chelsea on the roof of Wren's Royal Hospital, at Putney near the Telegraph Inn and at Coombe Warren in Kingston-on-Thames.

Never meant to be permanent, the network was in fact intended for use only until the end of the Napoleonic Wars. But with just four men per station (each overseen by a naval officer) it rapidly proved to be an extremely efficient and economical means of sending messages, reducing the time taken to just a few minutes and thus effectively guaranteeing its own survival.

Of the four operators, two would have been so-called glassmen, watching through telescopes for a signal from either of the neighbouring stations. The remaining two were the ropemen responsible for physically tugging on the ropes to operate the shutters relaying the message further up or down the line. The obvious drawback was that it could only be used in daylight hours, typically for six hours a day, and, of course, localised mist or fog would require individual stages to be covered instead by men on horseback.

On 6 July 1814, one of the more famous signals was sent down the line, when (with Napoleon banished to Elba) the stations were ordered to 'immediately discontinue'. When Boney landed back in France the following May, however, the link was quickly re-established and, after the victory at Waterloo, the Admiralty confirmed its plans to establish a more permanent link using semaphore, which is to say moving arms rather than shutters.

This new technology meant that each station would now have a crew of just two, a naval lieutenant and a handy- or signalman, many of whom were retired sailors. But, before long, technology played its hand once more and the mechanical method was rapidly superseded by a combination of the railway and the electric telegraph. In 1847, communication wires were laid alongside the rails of the London and South Western Railway to Gosport and the Royal Clarence Yard, and then by underwater cable across the harbour to HM Dockyard Portsmouth. Finally, on New Year's Eve 1847, the signalling station crews were stood down for the last time.

Unfortunately none of the London stations now survive in anything approaching their original forms, but one of the outlying stations can be seen at Chatley Heath near Cobham in Surrey and is open to the public.

QUEEN'S CHAPEL
MARLBOROUGH ROAD, SW1

Controversial Gift to a Catholic Queen

Bringing sixteenth-century Italy to seventeenth-century England as a gift for a Spaniard, but eventually made over to a Frenchwoman, the country's first Classical chapel was designed by Inigo Jones for Charles I's intended bride. When negotiations with the representatives of the Spanish Infanta faltered, however, work was suspended until 1626 when he successfully married Henrietta Maria of France instead.

The difficulties in 1623 had arisen chiefly because the traditional religious rivalries left the Spanish authorities unconvinced by promises from Charles that the Infanta could have sole charge of their children for the first twelve years, her own chapel, and a bishop and twenty priests all exempt from English law.

Fortunately for Charles, Henrietta Maria's spiritual guardians were easier to persuade. Even so, similar problems over her Catholicism meant that, together with a dozen monarchs and consorts in English history – from Matilda in 1126 to Edward VIII in 1936 – she was never actually crowned.

Henrietta Maria at least got her chapel, though, a building which together with the architect's other iconic, white or light-coloured buildings – the Banqueting Hall of 1619, the Queen's House, Greenwich (1616–35) and St Paul's in Covent Garden (1631–8) – must have conspired to make the mellow brick jumble of Tudor London look very old fashioned indeed.

That said, of course, at the time of its completion the chapel would actually have been an integral part of this same jumble, being attached to Henry VIII's 'goodly manor' at St James's until the driving through of Marlborough Road as a public highway in 1856 left it isolated on the opposite side of the street.

Unsurprisingly, given that it was built by a Protestant king for a Catholic queen, the chapel has paid host to a wide diversity of different worshippers over the years – not just the Queen Consort's Catholic masses, although these were certainly enough to outrage many of her husband's subjects, but also Dutch Reformed services for William and Mary, Lutheran services for several generations of Hanoverians, even Danish rites for Queen Alexandra. To further confuse the situation, from the eighteenth to the early twentieth century even the name was changed to the German Chapel Royal.

Not much else has altered over the years, however. The delicate pale-green and white colour scheme, with its Portland stone quoins, for example, dates from the earlier part of the seventeenth century. And inside, while a certain amount of refurbishment was carried out for another Catholic royal, Catherine of Braganza between 1662 and 1680, it is still a perfect Classical double cube, 110ft long and 55ft wide. It is also surprisingly elaborate given the refreshing simplicity and purity of the exterior.

Best of all, the interior is lit by a full-width Venetian window – another first for England – and, with a gallery for the expected royal pew, its intricate coffering, vaulting and carving can be enjoyed by the rest of us as well as the royal family. During the summer months, the chapel traditionally welcomes passing members of the public for morning prayer.

SPENCER HOUSE
ST JAMES'S PLACE, SW1

No Pretentious Palladian Hybrid

A fine example of the historical complexities of private landholdings in the capital, Spencer House is owned by the Crown (see p. 222) but has been leased to the Earls Spencer for more than 250 years, and is now sublet to Lord Rothschild, who has spent several millions restoring it for one of his companies.

Another spectacular rarity – an aristocratic palace overlooking Green Park, and like Bridgewater House strangely hidden away in the heel of a tiny cul-de-sac – it was originally designed for the first Lord Montfort, with the plans only being taken over by John Spencer in 1755 when Montfort shot himself dead.

The architect was John Vardy, a Palladian who was heavily influenced by William Kent and Lord Burlington. For what, by any standards, now looks like a superb site, he created a deceptively complex design which, despite an oversize pediment, appears light and almost festive when viewed from Green Park, even if Sir John Summerson reportedly thought the finished result little more than 'a pretentious Palladian hybrid'.

Unusually its principal façade overlooks the park rather than the entrance, perhaps because in such a narrow street it is impossible to get a really good vantage point from the pavement; in any event the design is also constrained on this side by its immediate neighbours.

The interiors were similarly left to James 'Athenian' Stuart, newly returned from Greece, with the result that the Italian house, as a pioneer of neo-Classical design, was almost certainly the first in London to have accurate Greek detailing inside. It was modified later, though, by Henry Holland, and again by the Victorian architect Philip Hardwick in the 1840s.

By 1895, however, the Spencers had decamped to Northamptonshire and Althorp, and their London residence was let to a diverse range of tenants. These included their kinsman the Duke of Marlborough and his wife (the former Consuelo Vanderbilt), the Ladies' Army & Navy Club, and, when their own premises in nearby King Street were hit in the blitz, Christie's the auctioneers.

The most significant, however, has been RIT Capital Partners plc under the chairmanship of Lord Rothschild. This company has overseen a mammoth restoration project designed to restore the interior to its pristine original form, re-hanging the walls with appropriate paintings (some lent to the enterprise by HM The Queen) and furnishing the house in an appropriate style.

Now chiefly offices, but with many of the state rooms made available for banquets and balls, Spencer House is also open to the public on most Sundays throughout the year. The closest thing London has to an unspoilt eighteenth-century private palace, it is not to be missed.

ST JAMES'S SQUARE
ST JAMES'S, SW1

One Queen, Six Dukes, Seven Earls

With the first of the great West End squares (and the best preserved of them all), Henry Jermyn, Earl of St Albans, sought to create an exclusive suburb convenient for St James's Palace comprising a mere twelve or thirteen 'great and good houses, fitt for ye dwellings of Noble men and other Persons of Quality'.

But even with his friendship with Queen Henrietta Maria (and a generous grant of land from her husband Charles I), his idea ran into trouble immediately. Unlike their European counterparts with their spacious, Parisian *hôtels* and Florentine *palazzos*, it seemed that country-minded English aristocrats simply weren't interested. Instead they were happy to make do with terraced houses, albeit rather grand ones, when spending time in London.

Jermyn quickly modified his plans accordingly, subdividing the square to create twice as many lots, which he then passed on to builders who were keen to erect something suitable for the rich, titled and otherwise well-connected types he knew would value proximity to the King.

This worked so brilliantly that, granted an English dukedom in 1682, the Irish Duke of Ormonde took a house there immediately. ('How ill it would look', said his son, 'not to have a house there now.') Soon indeed the square was thronging with no fewer than six dukes and seven earls, while celebrated architects active there included Sir John Soane, Nicholas Hawksmoor, John Nash, Robert Adam and Sir Edwin Lutyens. Today, however, of the original houses only the Duke of Kent's survives as planned, the Naval & Military Club at No. 4 enjoying not just his house and spacious courtyard garden but also a complete mews house at the back.

Meanwhile the square itself, while still technically privately owned by its occupants, provides a uniquely green amenity for weary visitors to the West End. Here one can see a fine statue of William III, complete with a representation of the molehill over which his horse stumbled with fatal results (the anniversary of which was marked for many years by Bonnie Prince Charlie's men, each drinking a cheerful toast to 'the little gentleman in black velvet'). But it's also worth strolling round the square itself, not just to see the buildings (most of which are Grade I or Grade II listed) but also the plaques, blue and otherwise, which tell their own stories.

No. 31, for example, was where Eisenhower formed his First Allied Forces HQ, while No. 10 was home to three different prime ministers: Gladstone, Derby and Chatham. Elsewhere one finds the childhood home of the future Queen Elizabeth the Queen Mother (at No. 20), and at No. 21 the home of not one but two mistresses of James II. No. 14 is still the world's largest private library, the London Library founded by Thomas Carlyle in 1841. And earlier still, No. 16 was the setting for a scene straight out of history when Major the Hon. Henry Percy arrived at a ball, bloodstained and exhausted, to lay the French colours at the feet of the Prince Regent and declare an allied victory on the field at Waterloo. Hollywood couldn't have done it better.

WESTMINSTER SCHOOL
LITTLE DEAN'S YARD, SW1

A Shilling a Day for Boarders

With buildings dating back more than 900 years, and later contributions from such outstanding talents as Wyatt and Lord Burlington, Westminster School has its origins in an early medieval establishment for the training of clerks attached to the pre-Conquest Benedictine Abbey.

In this connection, a Royal Charter still in the care of the abbey makes reference to buildings in 'the terrible place which is called Westminster', and is thought to have been granted by King Offa of Mercia in AD 785. Today, though, these historic school buildings – hemmed in on all sides, thereby limiting any chance to expand – offer a uniquely rich and rewarding part of the abbey precincts for the casual explorer.

The room known as School, for example, dates back to the end of the eleventh century and was originally part of the old monastic dormitory. For nearly 300 years, from 1602 onwards, the entire school was taught in this single space, the upper and lower schools kept apart by a curtain slung from an iron bar down the middle of the room. The bar can still be seen and, at least for the last 250 years, a pancake has been hurled over it each Shrove Tuesday. The child who is lucky enough to catch and keep hold of the largest scrap (after a fairly raucous scrum) is traditionally rewarded with a gift from the Dean of Westminster – originally a guinea, although these days he or she is more likely to receive a book token.

The pupils' refectory, known as College Hall Cloisters, is another ancient structure – completed in 1376, it would have been the Abbot's state dining hall – but architecturally the star of the school is probably Ashburnam House, which Pevsner acknowledges is 'the best example in London of a progressive and stately mid-seventeenth century house'.

Probably the work of John Webb, a pupil and son-in-law of Inigo Jones, its unexpected lack of symmetry reflects the fact that it was built on to a much earlier structure, the red-brick façade actually concealing walls of fourteenth-century rubble from the old Prior's Lodging. Traces of this can still be seen inside and out, but the chief beauty of the building is the sumptuous plasterwork in the staircase hall, an apartment which unlike so many of the school buildings has mercifully remained free of carved, schoolboy graffiti.

Also of note is the dormitory block or College. Originally designed by one of the school's more famous former pupils as a replacement for one housed in a medieval granary, in the event Sir Christopher Wren's scheme was actually executed by Lord Burlington and completed in 1730. He modelled his work on Palladio's studies of the Roman baths at Agrippa, perhaps also on the cloister at San Georgio Maggiore by the same hand. But, unfortunately, it was badly damaged in the Second World War and now, with the ground-floor colonnade glazed rather than open, the building looks somewhat less distinguished than in reality it is.

CHELSEA PHYSIC GARDEN
SWAN WALK, SW3

Britain's Oldest Rockery

Second only in seniority to a similar establishment founded at Oxford half a century earlier, Chelsea's secret garden was created by the Society of Apothecaries in 1673 on land the livery company had originally leased in order to build a boathouse for their ceremonial barge.

Within less than a decade it was well established as a physic garden instead – England's first cedar tree was planted here in 1683 and survived until 1903 – and in 1772, after purchasing the manor from Charles Cheyne, Sir Hans Sloane granted 4 acres to the Society in perpetuity for just £5 a year. His grant required them merely to maintain it 'for the manifestation of the glory, power and wisdom of God, in the works of creation' and to supply the Royal Society, of which he was president, with 2,000 rare plants to be presented at a rate of fifty per annum.

Still very much active in the field of botanical research today, the garden, with its more than 5,000 different species, is said by the workforce to enjoy a slightly warmer microclimate thanks to the proximity of the river. It can also claim a number of important 'firsts' in addition to the aforementioned cedars.

For example, Britain's first greenhouse and stove were installed here in 1681. Just three years later, when diarist John Evelyn (1620–1706) visited, it had its own underground heating system too: 'the subterraneous heat conveyed by stove under the conservatory all vaulted with brick so as [the gardener, Mr Walls] has the doors and windows open in the hardest of frost'.

Chelsea is also home to the earliest rock garden in the country, now Grade II listed, which was assembled in 1773 using building stone reclaimed from the Tower of London, along with fused brick and flint, and basaltic lava presented by Sir Joseph Banks PRS (1743–1820) after his successful trip to Iceland the previous year. Later still, it played a leading role in establishing India's extensive tea plantations, the erstwhile curator Robert Fortune in 1848 using a form of miniature, ocean-going greenhouse developed here to transport *Camelia sinensis* seedlings from China to the subcontinent on behalf of the Honourable East India Company.

Even so, the garden remained all but unknown to many in the borough for its first 300 years, although since 1983 it has been open to the public during the summer months.

RED HOUSE
TITE STREET, SW3

Radical but Classical

Conforming in terms of its layout to the Palladian ideal – with their higher ceilings the principal entertaining rooms occupy most of the first floor like a *piano nobile*, while the servants are housed in the basement – the aptly named and somewhat enigmatic Red House could scarcely be more different in terms of its dramatic if slightly box-like appearance.

It has, for example, a highly formal façade, yet a surprising one too, even a little weird. Not just because it is so plain and undecorated compared to its typically frilly Chelsea neighbours, but because the choice of materials – most obviously the strange but beautifully jointed French red limestone specified by architect Tony Fretton – makes one wonder what the planners were thinking of when they permitted such a severe and singular-looking structure to replace two others in this otherwise architecturally quiet (if slightly dull) riverside street.

The geometric façade with its unusual bronze windows is also strongly Palladian in its symmetry, although this is by no means absolute. At the same time, the face it presents to the street is quite forbidding and, compared to the other, mostly nineteenth-century houses, almost fortress-like – this despite the large central window and the unexpected strands of vegetation waving cheekily over the parapet to passers-by beneath.

In fact, the plants are perhaps the biggest clue to the surprising practicality and family friendliness of Fretton's idiosyncratic design.

The Red House, while clearly highly stylised and quite uncompromising in both concept and execution, nevertheless manages to incorporate not just generous entertaining spaces and flexible family areas, but also the aforementioned staff flat in the basement, a spacious double garage (unusually located dead centre) and at roof level a terrace with a hot tub, a tropical glazed hothouse and – quite obviously – superb views across London and the nearby river.

ROYAL HOSPITAL, CHELSEA
ROYAL HOSPITAL ROAD, SW3

Looking to establish a hospital in London for old or wounded soldiers, Charles II took as his model the Hôtel des Invalides in

Paris. The Royal Hospital was built on the site of 'Controversy College' – the Dean of Exeter's widely ridiculed and ultimately unsuccessful theology school (which, when it failed, was used to hold Scottish and Dutch prisoners of war).

The idea was actually the Paymaster General's, and the design Sir Christopher Wren's, but when the initial intake of 476 veterans first entered the buildings in 1689 they saw pretty much what we see today – or what its near neighbour Thomas Carlyle described as something 'quiet and dignified and the work of a gentleman'.

Since Wren there have, of course, been a few minor alterations: Robert Adam was here on and off from 1765 to 1782; Sir John Soane added some stables in 1814; and Quinlan Terry is even now working on a new infirmary. Nevertheless the 420 or so 'In-Pensioners' (as they are correctly termed) are still granted their own small and delightfully old-fashioned wooden cabins within the mellow red-brick wings, each with a plaque by the door identifying the occupant by name, age and rank. All are immediately identifiable too, being still required when in public to wear their highly distinctive eighteenth-century uniforms – blue in winter, red in summer – with a tricorn hat provided for special occasions.

It's possible to visit the cabins too (although an invitation from the incumbent is required to see inside one of them) as well as the chief glories of the hospital, namely the hall and chapel. The former features a vast portrait of the founder on horseback by Antonio Verrio, after which a visit to the small museum detailing the exploits of some of the occupants is a must.

Mind you, the welcome peace and quiet of the courts (except during the Flower Show, obviously) belie the hospital's occasionally riotous history. In 1852, for example, several people were crushed to death here by the crowds who came to pay their respects to the dead Duke of Wellington. (His Grace lay in state at the hospital for more than a week.) And half a century earlier, after failing to retake Montevideo, General Whitelock was formally cashiered by a court martial convened here in the hall.

In the grounds too, there is evidence of another imperial fiasco, namely the memorial to the fallen of Chilianwalla. A tall granite obelisk carved by Charles Cockerell, this was put up in 1853 'to the memory of 255 officers, non-commissioned officers and privates of the 24th Regiment'. Four years earlier they had all paid the ultimate price during what was to prove the costliest single engagement during the entire campaign to conquer India – and one that, these days, one hears remarkably little about.

FULHAM PALACE
BISHOP'S AVENUE, SW6
England's Largest Moat

An episcopal palace on land originally gifted in AD 691 to Erkenwald, Bishop of London, whose successors were still living here an incredible 1,280 years later.

In Erkenwald's day it would have been one among many of his country estates and for several centuries was surrounded by the country's largest moat. In 1856, the architect Sir Arthur Blomfield suggested this had been dug by Danish marauders keen to defend their latest territorial gains; more recent excavations point to Roman origins. In any event, it enjoyed the useful amenity of direct access to the Thames, but was eventually filled in. In fact, this was done as recently as 1921

– a great loss to London, as its extent is now estimated to have been an impressive 1,200 by 1,300ft.

Sir Nikolaus Pevsner dismisses the complex of surviving buildings as 'far from spectacular, a manor house, not a palace'. But most visitors these days would disagree, one suspects, particularly the locals who sensibly make good use of the amenity offered by the adjacent park.

For first-time visitors, its charm relies not simply on the whole place being such an unexpected find hidden behind the trees in an inner London suburb. It also includes the borough's only Grade I-listed building and furthermore offers visitors a rich variety of different building styles and periods on the one site. These include the large yet intimate courtyard known as the Fitzjames Quadrangle, with its mellow red and deep purple brickwork of *c.* 1510, and at the other end of the scale (in every sense) this picturesque (if slightly spooky) gate lodge which with its decorated piers was built some 300 years later.

To one side of the recently restored courtyard is the Great Hall, its highlight the rich heraldry of sixteenth- and seventeenth-century stained glass, and a screen brought here from the Hall of Doctors' Commons, a defunct college of advocates near St Paul's. This was added to by Bishop Terrick, who favoured a Gothic style, although his castellations were later removed. In 1867 further, less sensitive additions were made in the form of a new chapel by William Butterfield.

The significance of Fulham Palace does not stop at its buildings, however, for the gardens are equally impressive. Originally planned and planted by Elizabeth I's Bishop Grindal, they have been added to by many of his successors.

In particular, there are the aforementioned trees, many of which are highly rare (for London) and include several unusual specimens such as tamarisk and tulip, black American walnut and Virginian oak, ilex and cork. Nor was the collection assembled without considerable forethought. Indeed, as early as 1680 Bishop Compton was prevailing upon one of his missionaries to send back new plants from the American colonies, and received by return from John Banister a specimen of *Magnolia virginiana*, Britain's first.

COALBROOKDALE GATES
KENSINGTON GORE, SW7

Relic of the Great Exhibition

As technically ingenious as one might wish of something left here after the Prince Consort's Great Exhibition, these 60ft-wide gates were cast in a single piece at Coalbrookdale in Ironbridge, Shropshire.

Authentic pioneers of the Industrial Revolution, their Quaker makers the Darby family were to iron production what Richard Arkwright had been to textiles or James Watt to steam engines. Best known for building the world's first cast-iron bridge (across the Severn) and, with no fewer than five generations contributing to the more efficient manufacture of better and better grades of iron over more than 150 years, it was perhaps unsurprising that by 1851 the company they founded was keen to be associated with the Great Exhibition in Hyde Park. A celebration designed to showcase Britain's technological achievements and industrial and economic superiority to the rest of the world looked tailor-made for them.

Hit particularly hard by a steep decline in its normal business following the defeat of Napoleon, the company had only recently moved into decorative cast iron but, as the world's largest foundry, it produced a number of exhibits for the event, including fountains, sculptures, candlesticks and plaques.

By far the largest, however, were these ornamental gates. Produced under the direction of designer Charles Crookes, they were originally made to stand at the entrance to the north transept of the Crystal Palace, thereby signposting to the more than 6 million visitors who attended the exhibition the entrance to what was in effect Coalbrookdale's own, private display area.

So impressed were the Exhibition Commissioners, however, that, once the show had closed, Abraham Darby IV – who was destined to be the last family member actually to manage the company – was asked to re-erect them at the entrance to Kensington Gardens. Unfortunately, John Bell's iron fountain 'Boy and Swan', which was displayed alongside them in 1851, has since been removed to Shropshire's Museum of Iron, but the legend 'Cast at Coalbrookdale' can still be seen running along the base of the gates by anyone who cares to look.

LOTS ROAD POWER STATION
LOTS ROAD, SW10

Powering the Underground

This is an authentic Edwardian powerhouse built in 1902–05 to provide electricity for London's new Tube lines. The promoters of the scheme were on the one hand applauded for removing smoke from the tunnels by using electric trains, but on the other criticised and even sued for discharging it over the painters and parents of bohemian Chelsea.

James Whistler and others strongly objected to the ruination of the panoramic view of Chelsea Reach that had been immortalised by Turner. Parents were similarly up in arms because the pollution was soon drifting over an adjacent school and playground. *Punch,* meanwhile, helpfully suggested hoisting an equestrian statue of local worthy Thomas Carlyle to the top of the power station's four tall chimneys.

In the end, however, progress prevailed and, while today only two of the 275ft chimneys survive, Lots Road still stands proud over the river as the world's oldest thermal power station, and almost certainly the first steel-framed building in Britain.

It is truly immense too, with 220 concrete piers supporting brickwork on a German steel frame, the whole building some 453ft long, 175ft wide and 140ft high to the apex of the main boilerhouse roof. Inside, the original sixty-four boilers drew cooling water from an artesian well nearly 500ft deep, while also sucking in 50–60 million gallons a day from the Thames via a single pipe wide enough for a horse to walk through.

At first powering just the District Line, the station hoovered up 500 tons of coal a day as well, a reserve of 15,000 tons being stored for this purpose in unattractive bunkers by the station's own wharves. But as the Tube network expanded, so did the demands put on Lots Road. Those same bunkers grew to accommodate an additional 28,000 tons of coal, before the station switched over to oil and then to natural gas to power eight spanking-new Rolls-Royce Avon turbines.

Eventually, however, even these big numbers no longer made sense, not least because electricity could be more cheaply obtained from the National Grid than from London Underground's own generators. Similar calculations, and the fact that the power station's potentially attractive riverside location was now so much more valuable to developers than to the Underground, meant that the writing was on the wall for Lots Road, and before long it ceased generating.

Accordingly, at the time of writing, the next phase in its development is already well under way and, as part of a £500 million scheme designed by Sir Terry Farrell, its new sponsors are setting out to reclaim an area of Chelsea which has been largely hidden from the public for more than a century. What this means in practice is that, albeit with a promise of improved access to the river and a great deal of public open space around Chelsea Creek, yet another piece of post-industrial Britain is – surprise! – being reborn as luxury apartments.

SOUTH-EAST LONDON

COUNTY HALL
WESTMINSTER BRIDGE ROAD, SE1

Monumental, Magnificently Located

This building is every inch an Edwardian, although exceptionally long delays in its construction meant that there was a George on the throne when the first phase was considered ready for occupation, another one by the time the famous colonnaded crescent was in place on the river façade, and our own Queen Elizabeth by the time the whole project was finally signed off in 1963.

Since then, of course, the builders have been back at County Hall once again, this time remodelling the former home of the London County Council into an hotel, arts and entertainment complex on what remains one of the most magnificent sites in the whole of central London.

Inheriting a series of clearly inadequate offices at its foundation in 1889, after much prevarication the LCC alighted on this location diagonally opposite Parliament. For centuries, it had been occupied by a number of unsightly timber yards, wharves and warehouses, and, indeed, when excavation of the site commenced in 1909, the remains of a Roman barge were discovered in the mud before being removed to the Museum of London.

Ahead of this, however, a competition was held to find an architect for the massive project, with Edwin Lutyens (among many others) losing out to the largely unknown Ralph Knott, then aged just 29.

Never before had Knott been handed such a large or prestigious project, indeed nor was he to be afterwards as he died young, long before his masterwork was completed.

Nevertheless, when viewed from the north bank, his choice of an Edwardian Renaissance style works well, even if it has occasionally appeared a little bombastic. Certainly, it looks as if it was built to last, faced with Portland stone except at the base, where the architect specified granite like the adjacent embankment, giving the whole an appearance of great solidity and almost fortress-like impregnability.

A full 700ft long on the river side, County Hall always had two main entrances and today is best approached through the one which gives on to Westminster Bridge Road. Originally intended for the use only of Council members, this vaulted way has been compared to the work of Giambattista Piranesi (1720–78), taking the visitor through a series of archways and beneath an immense dome before emerging into the main central courtyard.

Now carefully landscaped by the hotel which occupies this end of the vast building, it makes a striking set piece and, as at Somerset House (see p. 33), one which for far too long was denied to ordinary Londoners.

GABLE COTTAGES
SUDREY STREET SE1

Another Lesson Ignored

Like an inner-city garden suburb on a pocket scale, a cartoon hamlet set around a minuscule village green, Gable Cottages is just one of housing pioneer Octavia Hill's (1838–1912) pleasant little oases in this busy but bleak part of south London.

The other is Red Cross Cottages in Redcross Way where Hill, persuaded that the working classes deserved a more human, civilised environment than that provided by traditional tenements, commissioned the church architect Elijah Hoole to create a row of emphatically picturesque cottages.

Completed in 1887 using a variety of different-sized gables, elevated bay windows and tile-hung façades, this offered not just soundly built, attractive housing but also community space and a community hall – an unusual and generous departure from the norm. Two years later, here at Gable Cottages, she allowed Hoole to go further still, combining half-timbering, decorated plasterwork and fanciful angled gables, and even an almost almshouse style of arranging the linked dwellings around a courtyard garden in a deliberate attempt to charm.

Clearly this is not great architecture: taken individually the dwellings are stylistically trite and lack interest. Viewed from our own time, there is also something slightly naïve and patronising about Hill's aims – for example, the Walter Crane murals she planned for the Red Cross Hall depicted 'Deeds of Heroism in the daily life of Ordinary People'. Hill herself had already noted that, even with the huge sums of money offered by benefactors such as Baroness Burdett-Coutts and the Countess of Selbourne (and grants of cheap land for affordable dwellings from the then Marquess of Westminster), more than thirty years of good works like her own had managed to rehouse a mere 26,000 people.

Nevertheless, as an exercise in communal housing such places are still important. Certainly, they are far more agreeable than the more or less contemporaneous Peabody type; and with Hill's aim clear – to make 'lives noble, homes happy and family life good' – they must surely have been far more congenial places in which to live.

One might also have hoped that, with Hoole's emphasis on individuality and his commitment to building houses rather than flats, the small-scale developments pioneered by Hill and her associates would at the very least have provided a valuable lesson in urban planning. Something, that is, to guide those post-war authorities which appeared so keen to destroy streets and communities and to replace houses with the monolithic blocks designed along so-called 'rational' lines.

But, alas, the authorities refused to be guided, and precisely this kind of heartless 1960s development now crowds on to Sudrey Street. The end result is that, more than a century later, Gable Cottages is still one of the more sought-after addresses in the neighbourhood. Quaint, a bit reactionary and almost too cute to be taken seriously, Hill's and Hoole's little houses are nevertheless precisely what the locals most want.

IMPERIAL WAR MUSEUM
LAMBETH ROAD, SE1

The Madness of War

Housed for a while in the former Imperial Institute at South Kensington – of which sadly nothing survives but T.E. Collcut's splendid but strangely invisible 287ft-high Queen's Tower – the museum was established by Act of Parliament in 1920 to collect, store and display material relating to the First World War.

The remit has since been expanded to include all conflicts involving British and Commonwealth troops since that date

and in July 1936 it moved here, into a building which for many seemed entirely apposite, being the central portion of a former insane asylum, the famous Bethlem Royal Hospital or Bedlam.

This in turn had its origins in the City, in the Priory of St Mary of Bethlehem, which had been established in 1247 on a site now obscured by Liverpool Street station. Founded by Simon Fitz Mary, a rich alderman and sheriff, by the fourteenth century the priory was used to house lunatics, many of the poor wretches being whipped and manacled to the walls, and until as late as 1770 being held up as a popular public attraction. This practice, while even more profitable when the hospital moved to larger premises at Moorgate, was finally abandoned when it was recognised that prurient gawpers 'tended to disturb the tranquillity of the patients [by] making sport and diversion of the miserable inhabitants'.

In 1815 the hospital, as it had by then become, moved again, into this building, designed by James Lewis (its dome and portico added later by Sidney Smirke), with extensive east and west wings that were unfortunately demolished in the early 1930s.

The criminally insane had by then been removed to Broadmoor, but over the years Bedlam's alumni have included a number of well-known names. Perhaps the most famous was A.W.N. Pugin, Barry's collaborator on the Palace of Westminster, and also architect of St George's Roman Catholic cathedral opposite this building. Others included Mary Nicholson who, in 1786, attempted to assassinate George III; Jonathan Martin, the York Minster arsonist; a couple of notable artists – Richard Dadd and the cat-man Louis Wain – and the novelist Antonia White.

When the hospital made its most recent move to Beckenham in Kent, Lord Rothermere bought the grounds. Naming them in memory of his mother, Geraldine Mary Harmsworth, he opened them as a park with the most notable feature being these two massive 15in naval guns.

Despite appearances, they are not actually a pair, but remain emblematic of the great days of British naval superiority. The one on the left, made by William Beardmore, was mounted in HMS *Ramillies* from 1916 to 1941. The right-hand gun, meanwhile, was made by Vickers, Son & Maxim and mounted in another *Revenge* class battleship, HMS *Resolution*, from 1915 to 1938. Later remounted in HMS *Roberts*, it took part in the D-Day bombardments during an attack on Houlgate Battery, east of Sword Beach.

SOUTH BANK LION
WESTMINSTER BRIDGE, SE1

Breaking the Coade

By far the best-known example of London's famous artificial stone – said to be the most durable and weatherproof of any such material so far invented – this 13-ton monster's more familiar name is in a sense a misnomer since the stone in question, in truth a form of white terracotta, was actually patented by Richard Holt in the 1720s. His Lambeth yard was only taken over by the unmarried 'Mrs' Coade forty years later, at which point, his patent having lapsed, she successfully modified his recipe with the addition of finely ground glass and prefired clay.

That was in 1769, after which, as the Coade Artificial Stone Manufactory, Holt's yard remained in business until 1840 when details of the stone's precise composition were somehow lost. Until that time, however, it was used to produce vases in which the most fashionable gardeners could raise their rare bulbs, before the range was expanded to include nymphs and sphinxes, statues, busts, keystones and other ornamental features for buildings.

The Coade stone lion was completed towards the end of this time, in May 1837 (it says so on one of its paws), and, after being painted bright red, was placed over the entrance archway of the Lion Brewery near Hungerford Bridge. By the time the brewery was demolished in 1949, the lion had survived the Blitz but disappeared, although it was recovered in time to grace the Festival of Britain on the South Bank. Two years later, at the King's suggestion, it was being removed once more, this time to the entrance of Waterloo station. Perhaps surprisingly for such a well-known feature of central London, it was installed in its current position only in 1966.

As for Coade stone itself, and somewhat unromantically, its secret 'lost' recipe has since been recreated perfectly in a laboratory at the British Museum. Nor is it quite true to describe the stone as indestructible. After all, if a man can make it a man can break it, and the lion has been discreetly altered over the years, most famously when a certain appendage was reworked after being considered too large once the lion came down from its high arch over the brewery gate.

ST MARY OVERIE DOCK
CLINK STREET, SE1

Landing Rights for Londoners

Nudging its way into the narrow streetscape, a floating replica of the *Golden Hind* is just one of the surprises for anyone wandering through this ancient part of south London. The boat in which Sir Francis Drake circumnavigated the globe, she sits on the water in the diminutive St Mary Overie Dock, a place which takes its name from one of the original benefactors of both St Thomas's Hospital and nearby Southwark Cathedral.

Awarded cathedral status only in 1905, before this date the latter had been the old church of St Saviour's and earlier still the chapel of the Augustinian Priory of St Mary Overie. This in turn was said to have been founded by a ferrywoman or the daughter of a ferryman – hence *overie*, meaning 'of the ferry' or 'over the river'.

At this time – possibly as early as the seventh century, but certainly before the Conquest – there were of course no bridges connecting this part of Southwark to the City, so ferries were at a premium and the potential profits high.

Certainly, in his *Survey* John Stow makes mention of 'a house of sisters', later 'a priory of canons regular' which had been founded by a maiden named Mary using the 'oversight and profits of a cross ferry or traverse ferry over the Thames'. It seems likely furthermore that the dock of the same name – where in theory at least local parishioners can still claim free landing rights – is the 'tideway where ships are moored' which is recorded in the Domesday Book.

There is more, however, including a colourful legend about Mary and her penny-pinching father. Apparently concerned at the rising weekly bill for feeding his household, the ferryman decided to feign death in order that his grief-stricken family would eat less. Unfortunately for him, upon hearing of his death the family and servants threw a party instead. Horrified at the cost the ferryman promptly sat up, was presumed to have been taken over by the devil, and was struck down dead by one of those present. At this point, says the legend, Mary's fiancé leapt up to stake his own claim to a share of the dead man's property, and Mary, understandably appalled at the display of greed and naked avarice, took her inheritance and gave it to the Church.

In time she was canonised, and by 1106 part of the Priory of St Mary Overie was hived off to become the Hospital of St Thomas the Martyr or, as we now know it, St Thomas's Hospital.

TRINITY CHURCH SQUARE
TRINITY STREET, SE1

South London's Finest Square

Centred on the ornate Italianate Holy Trinity Church of 1826, this extremely elegant late Georgian development is the most complete and best-preserved London square anywhere south of the river.

Developed by the Brethren and Corporation of Trinity House, the body charged with responsibility for England's lighthouses and lightships since at least 1514, it occupies land given in 1661 to provide income for seamen, their widows and orphans. It has survived mostly through luck but also careful management to become as it were the flagship of the surrounding Newington Trust Estate.

Work began in 1813 with the formation of Great Suffolk Street East (now Trinity Street), the square being built two decades later by a mason called William Chadwick. Obtaining the leases and permissions to 'form the Square round the new Church' (an innovation in urban planning at this time), he added three sides to the one formed by the houses already completed on Great Suffolk Street East before moving into the largest house at No. 29.

The industrious Chadwick was active elsewhere on the estate too, for example in Cole Street, where he built a chapel and some smaller houses; and in Swan Street, which was in a similar style but on an even more modest scale, although nothing but the Trinity Arms remains of the original. Today he is commemorated in the name of nearby Chadwick Square, which was completed in 2000.

Built as individual residences, most of the surviving buildings on the square have since been converted into apartments, some laterally and spread across two or even three house widths. Others have been entirely rebuilt, for example Nos 48–50, which were destroyed during the Second World War. Fortunately, retention of the façades or their careful restoration has done much to maintain the square's original style and integrity.

Chadwick's successful development naturally attracted imitators, most obviously the adjacent Merrick Square which was built by a local firm, Cooper and Bottomley, using plans from the Corporation's own surveyor drawn up in 1853. Comprising thirty-two slightly smaller houses and Holy Trinity Rectory, which was built in 1872 between Nos 16 and 17, this, together with the larger square, now forms the bulk of the historic estate, which has been an official Conservation Area since 1968.

Happily, Francis Bedford's magnificent church, characterised by its highly unorthodox placing of the giant Corinthian porch alongside the nave rather than at its end, has also prospered, though somewhat against the odds. By March 1971, it had already been standing empty for ten years (its defenders having managed to beat off a number of applications to knock it down to make way for a petrol station or ornamental gardens) and two years later it was gutted by fire.

The Disused Churches Committee was then fortunate to encounter the wife of the London Symphony Orchestra manager, who recognised that 'the acoustics are excellent and the church is in one of the quietest and most beautiful squares'. Restored and renamed the Henry Wood Hall, it is now a rehearsal and recording venue for the LSO and the London Philharmonic.

WINCHESTER PALACE
CLINK STREET, SE1

Episcopal Prostitution

Today an elegant 13ft rose window is all that remains of a bishop's palace dating back to 1109; it was itself only revealed by accident following a disastrous warehouse fire in 1814.

A relic of a medieval great hall that remained in use by successive bishops of Winchester for more than 500 years, it is part of a palace which at one time had an immense river frontage and which on its completion would have stood in a park extending over more than 70 acres. On the evidence of its undercroft, the hall alone would have been enormous (80ft by 36ft) and to the south would have been a large courtyard where today we find Winchester Square. As for its likely splendour, this can be gauged from the complex and lavish design of the surviving hexagonal window, which, after its restoration in 1972, even the normally dry Dr Pevsner conceded was 'gorgeous'.

On the same site was the bishops' private gaol, giving rise to the expression 'being in clink' which survives to this day, although the origin is obscure. The prison itself, however, was not rebuilt after being torched (along with the nearby Marshalsea) in the anti-Catholic Gordon Riots of June 1780, riots which are estimated to have caused more damage than Paris suffered in the entire French Revolution a few years later.

Until the mid-seventeenth century, the Winchester bishops were a major power in the land, with several castles and estates across the south of England. James I of Scotland accordingly elected to have his wedding feast in this one, after marrying Joan Beaufort at nearby Southwark Cathedral; the palace is also believed to be where Henry VIII first met his fifth wife, Catherine Howard.

In 1642, however, the episcopacy lost its power, whereupon the palace became a much larger prison for Royalist troops. Thereafter, when it was returned to the bishops at the Restoration, it was found to be in such poor condition that a decision was taken to develop the land for building and the bishops moved to Chelsea.

The 70 acres thus became what was in effect London's first suburb. More significantly, as the famous 'Liberty of the Clink', an area outside the jurisdiction of the City, the bishops' estate quickly became notorious not just for bull- and bear-baiting but also for its stews or brothels. So notorious, indeed, that with prostitutes banned from the City, anyone catching venereal disease in or around Bankside was said to have been 'bitten by the Winchester geese'.

That's a strange epitaph for the bishops' time in Southwark but, together with this fourteenth-century fragment – actually a section of the south wall of the hall, along with the west gable end on twelfth-century foundations – it is all that now remains of more than five centuries of power, patronage and prestige.

LESNES ABBEY
ABBEY WOOD, SE2

A Visible Lesson in Abbey Architecture

In the days before it was remodelled as an underpass, trams heading south from the Holborn–Kingsway subway (see p. 22) routinely announced their destination as 'Abbey Wood'. One suspects, however, that then, as now, few passengers on their way to or through Woolwich paused long enough to consider where the wood was or why it was so named.

That they didn't is perhaps all the more curious, because those same woods still exist, 200 acres of them, and take their name from an adjacent Arrouasian (later Augustinian) foundation that had been established on the site by Richard de Luci in 1178.

Lord of the Manor of Erith, de Luci endowed the house as an act of penance after supporting Henry II in the martyrdom of St Thomas à Becket. But unfortunately, and despite having estates on both sides of the Thames, it was never a particularly prominent or very wealthy house, not least because the canons were charged with the expense of draining and maintaining long stretches of the river wall.

In any case, by 1525 it was dissolved and the buildings razed, and upon being granted to Cardinal Wolsey the land was used to fund his new Cardinal College at Oxford (later Christ Church). After his fall from grace, later owners included William Brereton (who was himself executed for treason after becoming involved with Anne Boleyn) and Christ's Hospital. The school kept hold of it for some 300 years before handing the ruins over to the London County Council in 1930.

Today, while none of the walls rises to more than a few feet, from the excavations started by Sir Alfred Clapham before the First World War and continued in the 1950s, it is easy to see the precise layout of the original abbey.

With its chapter house, church and cloister, the kitchens, sacristy and slype (a narrow passing place, where guests could be received), it is what Pevsner called highly 'diagrammatic'. In other words: the low ruins of this sometimes forgotten Norman abbey, with only the odd, slightly more substantial chunk of doorway or stone bench poking above the mown grass and bluebells, provide the best possible guide to the layout, and hence the day-to-day functioning of a small monastic foundation of this time.

More than this, though, with the ugly Thamesmead developments visible in the distance, and the irresistible contrast between the ancient woods, these time-worn ruins and more recent human endeavours nearby (such as Sir Joseph Bazalgette's pioneering Crossness sewage pumping station), Lesnes Abbey and its immediate surroundings also present an evocative snapshot of the richness and diversity of a great city in which the only constant is continual change.

THE PARAGON
BLACKHEATH, SE3

Uniform Without, Bespoke Within

Converted into apartments after sustaining bomb damage in the 1940s, Michael Searles' enormously grand crescent originally comprised just fourteen immense Georgian mansions and looked magnificent. Linked to each other by plain white Tuscan colonnades, the ensemble proved from the start to be so ambitious as to almost bankrupt both the architect and the builder by the time it was completed in 1807.

Unusually, while seeking utter uniformity for the crescent's flawless Regency exterior, Searles set out to give would-be buyers the opportunity to create their own bespoke interiors – the actual walls could be arranged and rooms fitted out to suit any individual taste and budget. But, even building the houses as simple brick shells to accommodate this, his task proved much greater than anticipated, and indeed the scheme as a whole took more than ten years to complete once Searles had been granted the necessary development leases by the local landowner, John Cator (1728–1806).

A successful timber merchant and Member of Parliament, Cator had already diversified the family fortune into property and is credited with transforming the village of Beckenham in Kent into a substantial suburban town. A Quaker, he sought

to do the same at Blackheath, seeking to make an area of heathland, until then notorious for highwaymen and footpads, more attractive to upper-middle-class buyers.

To this end, he had acquired the estate and dilapidated Wricklemarsh House formerly owned by Sir Gregory Page Bt (see Bunhill Fields, p. 45). Paying a mere £22,250 in 1787 for more than 250 acres, he set about demolishing the Palladian mansion which, designed by John James, had reportedly cost its former owner no less than £90,000 to build. By selling the building materials, Cator was able to recoup two-thirds of his investment, whereupon the estate itself was broken up into small parcels, several going to Searles, who is also thought to have secured some pillars from the old house for his colonnades.

Of his many developments in south-east London – which include parts of South Row and Montpelier Row in Blackheath, the southern side of Gloucester Circus in neighbouring Greenwich, Marlborough House in Kennington and another, smaller crescent on New Kent Road – The Paragon is the masterpiece.

Comprising six pairs of houses and another, larger, central pair, each dwelling is of two bays plus two slightly concave bays, extending over five floors and with extensions into the single-storey colonnades. These are of Coade stone, as is the crescent's trim decoration, the finishing touches being matching lodges added to either end at some point during the mid-twentieth century.

As grand as anything Nash built closer to town, The Paragon was, in a sense, too far ahead of its time. The railways increased values in this part of London and eventually the gentrification of Blackheath began to put a gloss on SE3. But by then Searles' mansions had been split up and divided, and it seems unlikely now that even one of the fourteen will ever be restored to a single, substantial family dwelling.

THE COLONNADE
GROVE STREET, SE8

Remnant of the Royal Victoria Victualling Yard

As the sovereign's senior service, the Royal Navy is naturally proud of its ancient traditions – in comparison, say sailors, the RAF merely has habits – even if some of them cannot be accurately dated. For example, it is hard to place the famous rum ration earlier than 1844, not least because there was no official policy regarding spirits.

Instead beer had been the authorised drink of the British seafarer, at least until 1831 and despite the practical difficulties involved in loading and stowing (useful as ballast, half-ton butts were not easily embarked). Such difficulties encouraged the switch to rum and, at half a pint a day in the form of 'three-water grog' – meaning diluted with three-parts water – the Navy was soon consuming vast quantities.

Much of it came from here, the Admiralty's Victualling Yard, which was founded in 1742. Based on a much older establishment known as the Red House (1513), it remained operational for almost 450 years.

In fact, the Admiralty already had similar facilities close to Tower Hill, but these were becoming increasingly inadequate for a Navy which really was beginning to rule the waves; hence the decision to move to a 35-acre site situated to the north-west of the important Royal Dock (see p. 175).

Rebuilt after a series of disastrous fires in the 1750s, the yard was centred on two vast warehouses that can still be seen on the river today. Behind these were stores for every conceivable demand the Navy's ships might place on their provisioners – not just the usual sail- and mould-lofts, sawmills and workshops for capstan makers, coopers and wheelwrights, but also others producing clothing, tobacco, food and (of course) rum made on the premises.

Here a single vat is said to have been capable of producing an incredible 32,000 gallons of spirit at one go, while elsewhere in the yard slaughter- and pickling-houses, mustard and pepper mills, and numerous other factories, workshops and kitchens made up a vast, self-contained manufacturing enterprise on a scale that is hard to imagine today.

Nevertheless, with similar, if slightly smaller, facilities also established closer to the fleet at Gosport and Plymouth, and with the Navy gradually withdrawing from the Thames as we have already seen, the yard's eventual closure was inevitable. In the event, it survived, albeit in a reduced form, until as late as 1961, after which much of the site was cleared to make way for the GLC's aforementioned Pepys Estate. Happily, some of the better buildings were preserved, including the riverside warehouses of 1791 – now imaginatively converted into flats, a sailing club and library – and the elegant colonnaded houses shown here.

Originally providing accommodation and offices for the Porter and Clerk of Cheque, and latterly old people's housing, these look across a cobbled yard isolated from the road by a grand, carved gateway. The houses themselves were designed by James Arrow, Surveyor to the Victualling Office from 1744 to 1785, and, rather gratifyingly, the bollards shown are made from genuine Royal Navy cannon.

ROYAL DOCK
DEPTFORD, SE8

An Emperor in the King's Yard

Today there may be little to see, but from the time of Henry VIII to Queen Victoria this was a crucially important naval facility. Sir Francis Drake was knighted here when Elizabeth II came to inspect his ship, *Golden Hind*. Cook's *Discovery* was fitted out here before his final voyage to the Pacific. Even Peter the Great came and worked here as a carpenter, seeking to better understand shipbuilding and design. (He later claimed he would have enjoyed 'a much happier life as an admiral in England' than the one he actually had.)

London had been a significant port since Roman times, but the first Royal Dockyard was built at Portsmouth by Henry VIII. However, disputes with the Vatican over his divorce plans raised the threat of war with France and Spain, as well as highlighting the logistical difficulties of supplying ships at Portsmouth with cannon and shot from the Armouries in the Tower.

The Navy Board's solution was the construction in 1513 of two new yards on the Thames – conveniently close to the Armouries and to suppliers of rope, timber and canvas for shipbuilding, not to mention a ready labour force. Woolwich and Deptford were also handy for the palace at Greenwich, enabling the monarch, who took a close personal interest in naval matters, to watch the shipbuilding process, visit the finished vessels and even play at being captain before they set sail.

What became known as King's Yard was soon a very considerable establishment. With dry docks for building ships, and 36 acres of wet docks for fitting them out and maintaining them, it also had a large mast pond where oak, elm, beech, fir and later teak could be soaked and seasoned before being used – this can be seen as late as 1886 on Stanford's *Map of London*. There would also have been acres of storehouses for rigging and masts, workshops housing coopers and other artisans, and a ropeworks to supply the miles and miles of rigging needed for each man-o'-war.

Initially the dry docks were separated from the Thames by a wall of mud. This was removed piecemeal before each launch by scores of navvies, until 1574 when Deptford gained a set of floodgates.

By the 1800s, however, their position on a tidal section of the Thames meant the docks were silting up. With little room for expansion in the town, Deptford was also soon overhauled by dockyards such as Chatham and Plymouth, where larger-scale shipbuilding could be more easily performed. Activity here was eventually reduced to simple repair work, then finally in 1869 the King's Yard was closed and the docks filled in to enable the Foreign Cattle Market to move on to the site.

Later rebuilding has obliterated even this, although the corporation housing which now comprises the Pepys Estate is known to occupy the site of John Evelyn's Sayes Court. This was home to Tsar Peter, who rented it during his happy sojourn in London but, setting an unfortunate precedent for the area, his entourage vandalised it badly before moving on.

ELTHAM PALACE
COURT YARD, SE9

London's Art Deco Masterpiece

It is, reports one visitor to this most beguiling English Heritage property, 'the unexpectedness of Eltham Palace and what you find inside that makes it so special' – and he's not wrong there. Part medieval royal palace, part glamorous Art Deco showpiece, and just 7 miles from central London, the opulence of the Courtauld family's 1930s extension (complete with piped music, underfloor heating and a centralised vacuum-cleaning system) could scarcely provide a stronger contrast with the fourteenth-century moat and lofty Great Hall built by Edward IV.

In fact, Stephen and Virginia Courtauld were here for less than a decade, a brief footnote to the palace's 700-year history. But, before leaving for Rhodesia when the palace was requisitioned by the Army Education Corps, they made their mark, creating with the assistance of a talented but little-known Italian called Peter Malacrida what is generally acknowledged to be England's finest art deco interior.

Needless to say, it was controversial at the time, though not simply because it was on such a significant, historic site. In fact, when they arrived most of the buildings of the palace complex were abandoned and falling to pieces, and indeed had been this way for so long that as early as 1656 John Evelyn had found 'both the Palace and Chapel in miserable ruins'. Later, in 1827, Jeffry Wyattville had proposed actually pinching the roof – the third largest hammerbeam roof in the country – in order to reuse it at Windsor Castle. But, by 1930, HM Office of Works was on the case, and was busy repairing the Great Hall when the Courtaulds suggested they take over the project.

Granted a lease, they soon ran into objections to their plans to build over the ruins. There was also widespread criticism when the architects John Seely and Paul Paget restored the Hall and installed a minstrels' gallery – their style was described at the time as 'Hollywood Medieval' – while adding two new wings which were sniffily dismissed by *The Times* as looking like 'an unfortunately sited cigarette factory'.

Nevertheless, the house, when completed, was quite sensational. For the Courtaulds money was clearly no object, and the designer went to town with glossy black veneers, gold-plated bathroom fittings (obviously), great sweeping staircases – even without the portholes, the parallels with an ocean liner are impossible to miss – and as its centrepiece an immense, circular entrance hall complete with lavish marquetry murals incorporating rare and exotic woods.

Of course, today it seems incredible that anyone, even someone as rich and aesthetically competent as Stephen Courtauld, should be allowed to trample all over a royal palace. But without his money and vision Eltham today would be an historically important Hall but a less interesting place. As it is, it is an exemplar of craftsmanship and self-confidence, a fine tribute to the artisans of the 1930s and of the 1990s when English Heritage stepped in to restore it once again.

OLD ROYAL NAVAL COLLEGE
KING WILLIAM WALK, SE10

Controversy, Cruelty and Corruption

Giving visitors to Docklands perhaps the finest view London has to offer, and this correspondingly good one from the top of Greenwich Park, Wren's triumphant Baroque masterpiece on the site of Henry VIII's beloved Greenwich Palace was at first controversial, and later a place of cruelty and corruption. These days, however, it provides a grand and historic campus for one of Britain's youngest universities, and one which UNESCO acknowledges as comprising the finest and most dramatically sited architectural and landscape ensemble in the whole of the British Isles.

As he had done with his dozens of City churches, Wren designed the place for nothing. Agreeing not to charge a fee for the work, he set to when Queen Mary demanded that a new naval hospital be built after hearing of the plight of sailors returning, wounded but victorious, from the strategically important Battle of La Hogue, which in 1692 had returned control of the Channel to England.

With Hawksmoor assisting, his scheme was controversial because as first planned it would have obscured the view from the river of England's first Palladian villa. To preserve the integrity of Inigo Jones's authentically iconic Queen's House, therefore, the four blocks making up Wren's design were separated, an effect dismissed by Samuel Johnson as 'too much detached to make one whole', but which today, together with the Royal Observatory offset on the hill behind, makes for such a harmonious composition when seen from the water or the Isle of Dogs.

After Wren came Vanbrugh, who worked to the former's plans, then James 'Athenian' Stuart who rebuilt the chapel after a fire, and finally James Thornhill, whose decoration of the Painted Hall is today one of the college's chief glories.

As a hospital, however, it never enjoyed the same success as its near contemporary on Chelsea Embankment (see p. 145). Above all, it was perhaps too grand – a complaint was made in 1711 that 'columns, colonnades and friezes ill accord with bully beef and sour beer' – and this, along with rumours that the officers and staff were cruel and corrupt, resulted in the number of pensioners applying for places here dwindling alarmingly from a peak of 1,500.

By 1869, indeed, the hospital was empty and four years later the Royal Naval College was relocated here from Portsmouth. This moved again in 1998, merging with the RAF and the Army at a new Joint Services Staff College at Shrivenham in Wiltshire, and a new Greenwich Foundation took over the buildings and grounds for an initial period of 150 years.

With the University of Greenwich now installed, along with the Trinity College of Music, public access is happily much improved. The Painted Hall is of particular note: having been built as the hospital dining hall, it was also here, in 1806, that Nelson's body lay in state following his return from the Battle of Trafalgar. But perhaps the real high point is just wandering between the four blocks, with Greenwich Park stretching away to the south and, looking north, the starkest possible contrast courtesy of One Canada Square and the skyscrapers of Canary Wharf.

THE OVAL
HARLEYFORD STREET, SE11

London's Hanging Gardens

Lord's gets the plaudits but, for many, The Oval has enjoyed the more interesting history, this having started on 10 March 1845 when 10 acres of a former market garden were first leased for peanuts from the Duchy of Cornwall (see 224) by the Montpelier Cricket Club.

It was the scene of the first ever Test Match in September 1880, which England won by 5 wickets, and the inaugural FA Cup Final was played here too, when The Wanderers beat the Royal Engineers 1–0 in March 1872. More surprisingly still, the place that was to become world famous as the headquarters of Surrey County Cricket Club also did its bit for the war effort and, in 1944, was briefly converted into a prisoner-of-war camp.

Following the signing of that original 1845 lease – thirty-one years at £120 per year – 10,000 turfs were cut from Tooting Common and laid here at a cost of £300. Surprisingly, The Oval name was already in use, referring not to the ground but to the shape of the surrounding streets that had been laid out by then.

That same year, after a meeting in a nearby public house called The Horns, the first event staged here was a cricket match – the Gentlemen versus the Players of Surrey – but the ground was also regularly used for rugby and soccer, hosting every FA Cup semi-final and every final bar one between 1872 and 1892 at a time when the nascent Football Association and Surrey County Cricket Club shared the same secretary in journalist C.W. Alcock.

The Oval was also the opening venue for the first-ever tour of England by a foreign side (upwards of 20,000 spectators packed the ground to see the Aboriginal Cricket Tour of England in 1868) and, most famously, it was at The Oval in 1882 that Australia won the inaugural Ashes Test by 7 runs.

The first Test double-century was scored here too, by Australia's Billy Murdoch two years later. But perhaps that needs to be set against the unfortunate experience of his countryman Don Bradman – while making his last ever appearance in Test cricket in 1948, he was bowled out for a duck when all he needed was 4 runs to claim a remarkable career average of exactly 100 runs – and the recognition that England has traditionally done better here against Australia than at any other home ground, including Lord's.

For sporting historians, the ground naturally has more than its fair share of heritage, with an extensive collection of paintings in the pavilion, an excellent cricketing library and the famous 1934 Hobbs Gates named after John Berry ('Jack') Hobbs, the Surrey and England player who was the first professional cricketer to be knighted.

Its most outstanding feature today, however, and not just because of the huge contrast between it and the neighbouring local authority housing, is at the opposite or 'Vauxhall' end: a new and strikingly futuristic £25 million stand which, complete with its hanging gardens, was finished just in time for the Fifth Test in 2005.

DEPTFORD TOWN HALL
NEW CROSS ROAD, SE14

Edwardian Exuberance in Miniature

By the mid-seventeenth century, the growth of London was such that only a minority of its citizens lived within the City, and, as expansion continued, it rapidly became clear that administration of the outlying districts could no longer be left to parish vestries and justices of the peace.

Instead, increasing demands for better paving and policing, lighting, efficient drainage and so on led to the development of specific local authorities; as their powers and responsibilities grew so did their need for larger, better and purpose-built premises. As a result, and because the choice of premises was decided at a local level, by the 1960s the capital boasted at least 100 independent town halls which between them displayed a bewildering variety of different architectural styles.

These ranged from the Free Renaissance style of Hendon to the 1930s Modern of Wembley, from neo-Georgian in Beckenham to English Baroque in Woolwich, and from the Moorish-style ceilings of Tottenham to the sweeping, almost Scandinavian staircases of Haringey, the latter concealing atomic-bomb-proof concrete bunkers and an escape tunnel into the surrounding garden.

Perhaps the most unexpectedly exuberant, however, is this one in dreary Deptford, a wild Edwardian Baroque Revival affair which, despite occupying quite a tight site, somehow suggests generous dimensions. Sadly, however, with its exotic naval motifs and just a century old, it also now seems completely

out of keeping with this slightly seedy and run-down corner of
south-east London.

The town hall was completed in 1907 by Lanchester, Stewart
& Rickards, those maestros of civic architecture who were also
responsible for Westminster Central Hall (and the vast Portland
and marble wedding cake that is Cardiff City Hall). The naval
theme of course pays tribute to Deptford's long and illustrious
maritime history (see p. 175).

The motifs themselves are almost certainly the work of
Edwin Rickards (1872–1920), a lively conversationalist with an
acknowledged eye for detail. His friendship with the novelist
Arnold Bennett led to his appearance in at least three of the
latter's books, but his lasting monument is this one, with all its
swagger, splendour and sumptuousness.

This is most obvious on the street front, where there is
the lavish door casing shown here, as well as the line of naval
heroes: a quartet of admirals set between the windows of the
overhanging first floor. Similarly, within the tympanum of the
attic storey can be seen a recreation in stone of a battle at sea,
while the building is crowned by a clock turret and spirelet
complete with ship-shaped weathervane. Inside too, there are
crossed anchors, wrought-iron chains and trident-shaped
balustrading on the grand marble staircase – all quite delightful.

ROYAL ARSENAL
BERESFORD SQUARE AND DIAL SQUARE, SE18

Six Hundred Acres, and 4 Miles Round

By far the oldest, largest and most historic establishment of its kind in the world, Woolwich and its immense collection of solidly handsome military buildings are architecturally outstanding. Yet, despite their famous connections and sometimes fascinating history, they remain all but unknown to the majority of Londoners and as a consequence are rarely seen by visitors to the capital.

One would think, however, that the names of some of the early eighteenth-century buildings would alone be sufficient to bring visitors out this way. Add to that the likely fact that the splendid-sounding Brass Gun Foundry, Gun Bore Factory and Board Room and Saloon are the work of Sir John Vanbrugh and you realise that, were they anywhere but down here, these valuable additions to our national heritage would be thronged with visitors every day of the year.

All were built between 1717 and 1720 when the Arsenal followed Henry VIII's dockyards to the so-called Royal Warren. Relocated to what had hitherto been a small, quiet fishing village on the Thames, it came from Moorfields following the aptly named Great Explosion of 1716. An event 'occasioned by moisture in the moulds', this had been sufficiently destructive to persuade the government of the day that having such a potentially dangerous complex so close to the City was, to say the least, unwise.

Thereafter the Arsenal's expansion and prestige were more or less guaranteed. The first boost came during the American War of Independence, another during the Napoleonic Wars, and finally in 1805 it secured its royal prefix following a visit by George III. Indeed, what was Europe's largest military industrial complex stayed ahead of the game for some 300 years, with the Royal Laboratory attracting visits from many famous civilian pioneers and innovators including Marc Brunel, Joseph Bramah and Henry Maudslay; even Sir Henry Bessemer came here to test his steel.

By the First World War more than 80,000 people worked in its factories and storehouses, but decline eventually set in after 1945, when demand for armaments naturally dropped off dramatically. The ordnance factories were finally closed in 1967, after which half the site was sold off for housing.

A decade later, Woolwich as a whole was officially designated 'a disadvantaged area' and one where high unemployment was the norm. Fortunately, a rescue plan is now well under way, with massive regeneration on the site including 3,000 new homes, and hundreds of thousands of square feet of commercial and recreational space, including a cinema, bars, restaurants, shops and an hotel, together with parkland and a riverside promenade.

Inevitably, not all the conversions are quite as sensitive as one might have liked; and unhappily the site no longer includes 'Firepower', a really excellent museum which for several years charted the evolution of ordnance and artillery over more than six centuries. Maintaining a record of this important part of London's military history was a good thing, and its closure is to be regretted.

CRYSTAL PALACE DINOSAURS
THICKET ROAD, SE20

Stone Penge

Apparently concerned that something comprising 293,655 individual panes of glass, 4,500 tons of iron and 600,000 cubic feet of timber might not be sufficient to pull in the crowds, these twenty-nine prehistoric monsters were created as an important part of Sir Joseph Paxton's determined effort to make sure his Crystal Palace remained a popular attraction after its relocation in 1854 to south-east London.

Inhabiting a series of 'dinosaur islands' that were built in the park's artificial lakes, the immense models of several different types of long-extinct creatures – dinosaurs as well as mammals – were designed and sculpted by Benjamin Waterhouse Hawkins. But unfortunately, when the world's first Jurassic Park opened in 1854, it caused outrage to many Londoners by making a case for evolution over God, despite being nearly six years ahead of Darwin's publication of his ground-breaking *Origin of the Species by Means of Natural Selection*.

Paxton knew what he was doing, however, and before setting out he had assembled a team of eminent men and visionaries, including the respected anatomy professor Richard Owen. The first to coin the word *dinosaur* – meaning 'terrible lizard' – Owen worked alongside Paxton and Hawkins to create convincing representations of those monsters which had so far been identified. Further validation for this journey through 350 million years of evolution was ensured by the planting of ferns and suitable geological features intended to provide the right sort of setting for the monsters.

More recently the dinosaurs' original colours have been carefully researched and re-applied, while repairs or replacement of the models have been undertaken, including the creation of two new pterodactyls and a new limestone cliff.

Now, as a result, the Dinosaur Court (to give it its correct 1854 title) continues to thrill visitors both large and small. That said, there are unfortunately no plans yet to repeat the dinner with which a party of twenty-two distinguished men of science and letters celebrated the Court's completion. This took place in the stomach of a partly completed iguanodon on New Year's Eve 1853, the toast being the following:

> Saurians and Pterodactyls all!
> Dream ye ever, in your ancient festivities,
> Of a race to come, dwelling above your tombs,
> Dining on your ghosts!

Splendid stuff!

DULWICH GALLERY MAUSOLEUM
COLLEGE ROAD, SE21

No Parting, Even Unto Death

Attached to England's oldest public art gallery, owned and administered by the College of God's Gift at Dulwich, this singularly handsome building has its origins in an establishment founded by actor Edward Alleyn nearly 400 years ago.

Having accrued a considerable fortune as James I's Master of the Royal Game of Bears, Bulls and Mastiffs, in 1605 Alleyn paid £5,000 for the manor of Dulwich. Married, but without issue, he further decided to endow an educational establishment there and, wishing his foundation to rival the likes of Charterhouse, Merchant Taylors' or even Eton, he provided accommodation for fellows as well as 'alms-people'. When he died in 1626, Alleyn also bequeathed a collection of several hundred paintings to his new college.

Thereafter, and despite backing the wrong side in the Civil War – the fellows melted down their collection of silver to support the Royalist cause, and as a consequence had the Cromwellian quarter troops on them when their fortunes turned – the college prospered. Later still, Alleyn's (by now valuable) collection of paintings was augmented by a generous bequest of another 370 from the painter Sir Francis Bourgeois.

With many of these paintings truly world-class, the bulk of this later bequest had come via art dealer Noël Desenfans, who had acquired many from the famed collection of the Duc d'Orléans. He had been collecting for some years on behalf of King Stanislaus II, who intended the works to form the nucleus of a Polish national gallery in Warsaw. However, the country's partition in 1795 and the King's abdication made such a thing impossible.

With Poland gone from the map, split between Prussia, Russia and Austria, Desenfans and his wife shared a house with Sir Francis in England. Maintaining a curious *ménage*, which indeed has continued beyond the grave with the three of them still lying together in sarcophagi in a little amber-lit structure,

Desenfans first offered the collection to the Russian and later the British governments, but there were no takers.

Instead, following his death in 1807, they were left to Sir Francis with instructions that he was to see them settled on an appropriate institution. Once Dulwich had been selected (he counted several fellows among his friends) approaches were made to Sir John Soane to design an appropriate setting for the paintings.

Choosing to use London brick instead of the Portland stone which was then most fashionable, he created a severe yet harmonious box, cleverly top lit to throw light onto the white, unadorned walls. The effect was to illuminate the paintings without the aid of artificial light, but at the same time to avoid the damaging direct sunlight or irritating reflections that would have arisen had the architect equipped the gallery with conventional windows.

As a finishing touch, opposite the main entrance, Soane included the mausoleum. Based on an engraving of an Egyptian catacomb which had been published just two years after the death of Desenfrans, it is a sombre, though deeply lovely, place.

EAST LONDON

DIRTY HOUSE
CHANCE STREET, E1

Rubbish Reborn

What the *Guardian* called David Adjaye's 'massive corner slab', the Dirty House was built for artists Tim Noble and Sue Webster. Since then, coated in rough and thickly applied anti-graffiti paint with the colour and texture of plain chocolate fudge, it has become one of London's most challenging, even ugly domestic buildings.

But that said, the almost blank design of the façade represents quite an advance on Adjaye's earlier Elektra House in Whitechapel. Black, brooding, almost alien, that one lacked even a single window on the street side, though as a consequence of this (and like the Dirty House) it somehow manages to suggest peace and tranquillity in an otherwise visually very busy urban environment.

Strangely the charismatic Ghanaian denies that he is a classic minimalist, but there is certainly something stripped, pure, even quite naked about this particular live-work space.

In fact, with its two lofty studios, the Dirty House now forms part of London's newest artists' enclave. Rachel Whiteread's converted synagogue is next door, the gleaming White Cube Gallery is nearby, and elsewhere in the vicinity now known as the Shoreditch Triangle Antony Gormley and Michael Craig Martin both have new studios.

Adjaye himself, of course, has already built others for Chris Ofili and Jake Chapman as well as the new premises of Modern Art Inc, but the Dirty House is perhaps the most extraordinary.

193

The name was bestowed on it by Adjaye rather than by his clients and chimes in nicely with their work – particularly a 1998 piece called *Dirty White Trash (With Gulls)*, which was assembled from six months' accumulation of domestic waste, and another installation which used a collection of rubbish to produce a shadowy self-portrait projected on to the wall at the Royal Academy.

Adjaye's starting point for the building was a disused and much-decayed furniture factory, the sort of architecturally worthless structure most buyers would have knocked down simply to free up the site. For Noble and Webster, however, Adjaye chose to keep an old and crumbling brick wall and to incorporate this together with the existing openings into an otherwise all-new structure.

Finished in the aforementioned anti-graffiti paint, and with several of the windows weirdly flush-fitted with mirror glass, the effect is theatrical and unsettling. The front door, for example, is all but invisible, and with the upper row of windows set back to reveal the bulky, heavy mass of the wall, the house looks not merely secure – clearly a useful attribute in twenty-first-century London – but actually quite confrontational.

From a distance, it is true, but this effect is to a degree ameliorated by the delicate white 'lid' which appears almost to float on top. However, being set back and further softened by a few plants, this semi-weightless feature is all but invisible from the street below. As a result, the contrasting lid, above floor-to-ceiling windows for the artists' main, light-filled living area, provides little or no relief from the dark, brooding bulk of the building down below.

HAWKSMOOR'S LEGACY
CANNON STREET ROAD, E1

Blitzed, Burned and Bashed About

He has enjoyed a glittering career despite working in Wren's shadow and today is rightly revered. Even so, the buildings of Nicholas Hawksmoor, in particular his highly idiosyncratic churches, have enjoyed a far from smooth ride from their completion to the present day.

A contemporary account records for example how, at the consecration of St Anne's in Commercial Road, after the bishop had drunk 'a little hot wine and took a bit of ye sweetmeats', the clergy literally fought over the rest, engaging in fisticuffs, so keen were they to get their fair share. Of course, they may have just been hungry, for it is known that, when the great building was finally completed, the bill was so much greater than expected that the congregation no longer had any money left to pay the priests, let alone to buy them dinner.

Indeed, what Sir Simon Jenkins describes as 'a controlled explosion of architectural form' had a very shaky start. Formed in the shape of a Greek cross topped by a towering beacon, Portland stone pyramids and the highest church clock in the capital, it took a full twelve years to build, and even then parishioners had to wait another six before it could finally be consecrated.

Soon after that it was gutted by fire. Later still it was coldly restored by Sir Arthur Blomfield and then badly damaged again, this time in 1941 by enemy action. Sadly, though, just such a fate has been all too typical of the architect's other churches too, six of them having been created following Queen Anne's 'Fifty New Churches' Act of 1711 and paid for at least in part with a tax on coal.

Thus in Greenwich his Church of St Alfege with St Peter was built without the tower he planned (this later popped up here, on St George-in-the-East). It too was damaged during the Second World War and today is cruelly assailed by traffic. Similarly, his hugely self-confident Christ Church Spitalfields over the river, originally built to serve Huguenot refugees as the East End grew more crowded, was struck by lighting in 1841, then insensitively restored by Ewen Christian, and in our own time left to moulder for more than thirty years.

Finally to St George-in-the-East, with its stark, soot-stained white Portland stone, mammoth 160ft tower and refreshing lack of detail or decoration. For years this too languished, just another bombed-out shell, before it was chopped about in the 1960s in order to house a newer structure of a blander and far less distinguished design.

But the assaults on this one's noble fabric actually started far earlier than this. In the 1850s it was already being reported that there were riots on the premises, with men wearing hats and blowing horns in protest at the choice of incumbent, openly smoking pipes, bringing in dogs, and even throwing rubbish on the altar. Faced with such outrages, the rector eventually had a breakdown and quit, and the great St George's closed its doors in 1859.

LONDON HYDRAULIC POWER COMPANY
WAPPING WALL, E1

Heath Robinson Comes to Town

It's hard to imagine now but, for more than a hundred years (until the 1970s, incredibly), a company with its own private network of pipes and tunnels – nearly 200 miles of them, including one under the Thames which is large enough to drive a car through – was busy supplying pressurised water around the capital to power hotel lifts, theatre curtains and revolves, presses for hat-blocking, forging, flanging and stamping, even dockyard cranes.

London had hydraulic power companies before, of course – an accumulator tunnel can still be seen at the southern foot of Tower Bridge – but none was as successful, anywhere near as long lived or as extensive in its operations as the LHPC.

Running from Limehouse in the east to the Earls Court Exhibition Centre, from Pentonville Road across the river to Southwark and Rotherhithe, the vast majority of the company's conduits were pipes rather than tunnels, and generally less than a foot in diameter. But, significantly, all but 12 miles were manufactured using Victorian cast iron, and have proved to be of sufficiently good quality that, 130 years later, many are still in use today carrying fibre optics and other communications equipment around London.

Above ground too, some evidence of the company has survived, notably the ivy-clad Grade II listed building. Once charged with maintaining the pressure of the water at 600lb per square inch as it surged around the network, it is the sole survivor of six formerly operated by the company, the others having been by Blackfriars Bridge, at Bessborough Gardens in Pimlico, in the Rotherhithe and East India Docks, and by the Grand Union Canal in Islington.

To feed them, what had at first been called the Wharves and Warehouses Steam Power and Hydraulic Pressure Company was officially authorised to draw an incredible 25 million gallons of water a week from the Thames. Initially this was done by steam power, but in the 1940s, after sustaining some bomb damage, the switch was made to electricity.

By 1971, however, these extractions had fallen by 40 per cent or more, and staffing was down to just half a dozen men. Reflecting a decline in demand as the docks closed, the company was also hit heavily by the reduction of manufacturing capacity in the capital, and by the demolition of so many city mansion blocks which had previously relied on its services to power the lifts.

The location of these blocks can still be deduced, however, as can many other former customers, simply by looking out for distinctive square manholes on London pavements, each marked LHP. It is also possible to see some of the surviving pipework, for example where it crosses the Thames attached to Vauxhall, Waterloo and Southwark bridges.

WAPPING UNDERGROUND STATION
WAPPING HIGH STREET, E1

Brunel's First Underwater Tunnel

The Babylonians constructed a tunnel under the Euphrates river, the Romans ran one across the harbour at Marseilles, but in modern times the first tunnel to be successfully excavated underwater was the Wapping–Rotherhithe route running beneath this modern and quite hideous monolith.

Unusually horseshoe-shaped rather than circular, and some 1,300ft from end to end, Marc Isambard Brunel's tunnel was actually the third to be attempted beneath the Thames. The first two were defeated by quicksand, and this third one was achieved at the cost of only ten lives, albeit one a drunk who slipped and fell down the shaft.

An energetic genius and successful entrepreneur, the celebrated French exile had made his fortune manufacturing boots for the army and pulleys for the navy before Napoleon's defeat reduced demand for both and consigned him to a debtors' prison. It was there in his cell, however, that he had his greatest brainwave: his observations of how the common shipworm *Teredo navalis* used spoil from its excavations to shore up the burrow behind it suggesting to him a design for a new tunnelling machine, which he patented in 1818.

Using this to excavate this third attempt on the Thames, he realised, could link the manufacturing hub of Rotherhithe to the docks and markets north of the river without the need to make the 4-mile journey overland via the heavily congested

London Bridge. Accordingly, work started in March 1825 and by November the entrance shaft – which today forms the central hub of Wapping station – was completed.

Three months later, the excavations had reached the halfway point, but seepages, leakages and floods, a huge gas explosion and a bewildering array of exotic illnesses among the workforce began to undermine the whole project. What for *The Times* had started out as a great national enterprise thus rapidly became 'Brunel's Great Bore', and soon its creator began to fret too when his workmen began finding fragments of wood and china in the spoil, suggesting they were digging dangerously close to the river bed above.

In due course the tunnel gave way, the waters poured in, and Brunel succumbed to a stroke. He recovered slowly, work restarted and a banquet was held in the tunnel with loyal toasts to the King. But, in January 1828, the Thames rushed in again and, while two workmen died, Brunel's son escaped with his life only by being lifted by the force of the floodwater up the shaft and out.

It was to be a full fifteen years before the tunnel was completed but, lacking funds to construct ramps for carriages, the tunnel was even then accessible only to pedestrians who soon tired of the long, hard climb and returned to the ferry boats. Before long, the semi-deserted tunnel became the haunt of footpads and street-walkers, and only narrowly avoided conversion into a sewer. Eventually it was taken over by the East London Railway (which ran trains through it to Brighton), and subsequently by the modern Metropolitan Line.

WHITECHAPEL BELL FOUNDRY
WHITECHAPEL ROAD, E1

Gone But Not Forgotten

Established in 1570 – although a firm link has been established with Richard Chamberlain, who was active in 1420 as a 'bell-founder of Aldgate' – the modest Grade II listed premises at 34 Whitechapel Road have been responsible for many of the world's great bells, including Big Ben and America's famous (and famously cracked) Liberty Bell.

Even allowing for its formidable reputation, however, the survival of what is still a family-owned and -run firm is quite extraordinary. Remarkable too that it has remained in central London so many decades after any comparable heavy industry has collapsed or moved on. But then the Bell Foundry, with a history spanning the reigns of some twenty-seven English monarchs, is clearly a quite singular institution.

It was, for example, already pre-eminent in its field by the time of its move to Whitechapel from Houndsditch in 1583; very shortly afterwards it was busy casting new bells for the officers of Westminster Abbey, who remain regular customers 400 years later. It rapidly became an international enterprise too, initially by supplying a set of bells to Russia's new capital at St Petersburg (in 1747) and making its inaugural transatlantic sale just seven years later when America's first ever change-ringing peal was installed in Christ Church, Philadelphia.

In fact, its highly specialised operations have remained more or less unchanged ever since, but for a short break during the

Second World War. (Bell metal being so similar to gunmetal, for a few years manufacture switched to machine castings for the men from the Ministry as well as submarine parts for the Admiralty.) Today, as a result, at least 80 per cent of the business still involves the manufacture of church tower bells, carillon bells and the complete range of associated accessories such as frameworks, wheels and clappers.

The premises we see now bear that out too and date from 1670, just four years after the Great Fire. They were built on the site of an inn called the Artichoke, the lease of which was acquired by Thomas Lester – then Master Founder at Whitechapel – to meet the need for extra workshops and other accommodation as his business boomed. Happily, the cellars of the seventeenth-century roadhouse survive and are still used by the founders today.

For many, though, the most distinctive feature of the building is at ground level, namely the replica of the bell frame from Big Ben through which one steps to gain access from the street.

Consuming nearly 10½ tons of molten copper and more than 3 of tin, and taking twenty days to cool, its shape commemorates what is still, in nearly four and a half centuries of casting, the largest bell ever made in London. It is also the most famous one in the world, even if the name of its designer has all but been forgotten: Mr George Mears.

WILKES STREET
SPITALFIELDS, E1

Elegant Sweatshops

Weavers' houses, with their characteristically large attic windows to admit the maximum amount of daylight for those beavering away inside, are still not an uncommon sight in the north, but finding something similar in the heart of central London comes as something of a surprise.

That said, of course, Spitalfields – the name comes from a hospital and priory known as St Mary's Spital, founded in 1197 – has long been a veritable hive of light industry, and for a century or more was known for its weavers, particularly Huguenot craftsmen from France. They came here to escape the persecutions following the Revocation of the Edict of Nantes in 1685, and it was their skill, particularly with silk, which won the area its reputation for such fine and expensive work.

As a result, while the area was predominantly never anything but poor, a number of tall, elegant houses such as these – and similar terraces in nearby Fournier, Princelet, Hanbury and Elder Street being among London's oldest – bear witness to the fact that it was also home to many wealthy silk merchants, skilled master weavers and other successful tradesmen.

For a long time they and their workers were protected, and even assisted, by specific laws forbidding the importation of silk from France, so that, by the beginning of the eighteenth century, the area produced some of the finest cloth in Europe. Intended for both male and female clothing, this included figured silk brocades, damasks and velvets. Their pre-eminence gradually came to an end with the conclusion of the Napoleonic Wars, however, and while the work continued in Spitalfields it tended to be in these attic-level sweatshops rather than in the hands of skilled artisans.

Eventually the Huguenots moved on from Spitalfields, to be replaced by successive waves of new immigrants whose paths can be traced in the histories of many of the buildings still standing. Thus, for example, 19 Princelet Street was a Huguenot silk-weaver's home in 1719 before being refitted exactly 150 years later as a semi-secret synagogue. Similarly, the mosque now in Fournier Street, and used as such since 1976, was previously another synagogue, a Methodist chapel before that, and earlier still a Huguenot one, having been built for that purpose in 1743.

Fortunately, these and a good many other Georgian buildings, including houses standing in the shadow of the magnificent Christ Church Spitalfields, have somehow survived the area's many upheavals and changes of fortune. Some have now been beautifully restored by private owners who in the last twenty years or so have come to value the area for its proximity to the City as well as for its elegant architecture. Others, now glorious with the patina of age, have been repaired by the Spitalfields Housing Trust.

COLUMBIA MARKET
COLUMBIA ROAD, E2

A Dickens of an Idea

A well-meaning but misguided attempt by the philanthropist and banking heiress Baroness Burdett-Coutts (1814–1906) to save the costermongers from the streets, this mammoth rebuilding of a poor and squalid section of the East End followed a suggestion from her friend Charles Dickens. It quickly failed, however, not just because of opposing vested interests but also because many of the market men simply preferred their itinerant lifestyle and liked to be out on the streets.

Designed by H.A. Darbishire and built in a fashionable mock-Gothic style at the immense cost of £200,000, the market opened in 1869, by which time Lady Burdett-Coutts was already well known to the costermongers, generously having earlier provided stabling for their donkeys. (The first woman ever to be made a Freeman of the City, she was a prime mover in both the Royal Society for the Prevention of Cruelty to Animals and the new National Society for the Prevention of Cruelty to Children.)

This particular scheme, though, was altogether more ambitious than anything she had built for the donkeys. Planned as a vast open quadrangle and strongly ecclesiastical in appearance, it was surrounded by market buildings, a huge Gothic-style medieval cloth hall and a bell-tower, from which hymns sounded every quarter of an hour. It also incorporated the model tenements shown here, vaguely prison-like with their open staircases and galleries, and of a type now familiar across much of London – as the same Henry Darbishire was for many years also architect to the Peabody Trust.

The market itself was built on the site of 'an erasement of a vast number of vile dwellings' – possibly the very dustheap described by Dickens in *Our Mutual Friend* – an edition of the *Illustrated London News* at the time describing how 'a large part of the local population, at the best of times, is on the verge of pauperism'. As for the name, it came from the Bishopric of British Columbia, another recipient of its sponsor's largesse.

However, even with its modern facilities, room for an incredible 400 stallholders and no start-up costs, Columbia Market was never to pay its way and despite various attempts at reinvention (at one point it was handed to the City Corporation, which ran it as a fish market) it closed in 1886. Later let as workshops, it was finally demolished in 1958 despite protests, including one from Nikolaus Pevsner who called for it to be 'preserved at all cost'.

That said, while recognising it as 'easily the most spectacular piece of design in Bethnal Green', Pevsner was himself in no doubt that Columbia Market was also one of the great follies of the Victorian age. Replete with elaborate vaults and piers, decorated tracery, lofty, gabled halls and carved inscriptions urging stallholders to 'Be sober, be vigilant, be pitiful, be courteous', the money he felt might have been more usefully spent housing the residents more humanely and in much greater comfort.

GREENWICH FOOT TUNNEL
E14 TO SE10

Claustrophobic but Magnificent

Excavated in 1897 by the great Empire engineer Sir Alexander Richardson Binnie, the 1,217ft-long Greenwich Foot Tunnel opened in 1902, when it replaced a ferry which had been operating here since at least 1676. Once completed, it enabled south London dock workers to walk to work in the then thriving West India Docks.

There must have been thousands of them then, but these days, and despite the prominent pagoda-like domed entrances containing lifts and staircases, Greenwich Foot Tunnel and the one at Woolwich are probably the least-known tunnels in London to which the public has access.

Much of that, of course, is because even now, after hundreds of millions have been spent redeveloping the old docks, there is (besides the incredible view) little to tempt anyone in Greenwich to cross the river. This being so, one can only hope that this relative lack of use will not in the end be used by the authorities as an excuse to cut back on maintenance and then close the tunnel.

In fact, the Foot Tunnel is one of a pair running between the Isle of Dogs and Greenwich, the other being a conduit for cables from the hideous Deptford Power Station. Sir Alexander's is easily the more splendid, however, a triumph of Edwardian confidence and solidity with more than 200,000 glazed, off-white tiles lining the 11ft-diameter walkway, and a magnificent pair of spiral staircases snaking round matching mahogany-panelled lifts.

Appointed chief engineer to London County Council after a long and successful career on the subcontinent, Binnie also worked on the original, much larger Blackwall Tunnel. In its day this was the widest sub-aquatic tunnel in the world, taking more than seven years to complete, and despite its name consuming another million similar off-white tiles. For all that, however, his work is better seen at Greenwich, if only because when travelling on foot one has time to stop and look around.

Pedestrians may also notice a sign in one of the pagodas which still records the by-laws introduced by the LCC in 1903: 'No person may enter the tunnel in a state of intoxication [or] shall spit on or upon the tunnel or its approaches, stairs, lifts, passages, or other means of ingress or egress thereto or therefrom.'

Reading it now it is not hard to see why Binnie's masters were so proud of their tunnel: it looks tremendous as it dips down in the middle and then rises again as it passes under the middle of the Thames above. In fact the surface of water at low tide is at this point barely more than 30ft above, and it is said that, on the rare occasions a large ship passes overhead, those in the tunnel can actually hear the churning of its propellers. Fortunately the water has never actually broken through – as it did when Sir Marc Isambard Brunel was digging his tunnel across from Wapping (see p. 199) – although some reinforcement was felt necessary at the northern end when a German bomb fell nearby in 1941.

ORCHARD PLACE
LEAMOUTH, E14

Catch It While You Can

Sadly it won't be long before such places as this simply don't exist anymore, this particular one an eerily Dickensian and quite desolate spot marking the point at which the River Lea, after rising in Bedfordshire, finally reaches the Thames. It takes its name from Orchard House, later the Orchard House Tavern, which stood nearby until its demolition in the 1850s.

The necessary redevelopment of the docklands in the 1980s swept away a lot of the character as well as the squalor, and later the 2012 Olympics did likewise for much of the Lower Lea Valley. Happily, Orchard Place survives more or less intact, home to London's only surviving lighthouse, a lightship and their associated buoy sheds, as well as some funky live work spaces for artists and a truly panoramic view of this curving stretch of river dominated by O2 Arena on the opposite bank.

It is also notable because another of the more regrettable consequences of the docklands redevelopment has been the very considerable erosion of public access to the river. To a great degree this has been due to the construction of large residential schemes and gated 'communities' which have thrown up a barrier between the river and anyone living in the hinterland. Thus, for now, Orchard Place remains one of the few places where one can still easily reach the water's edge.

Even so, standing here in the early morning – a mug of coffee from the Fat Boy Diner in one's hand, and the noise of the traffic on the bypass present but pleasantly subdued – it is clear that few these days take the trouble to come here. It's also hard to appreciate just how busy this stretch of the river and riverbank must once have been.

In fact, as Trinity Buoy Wharf, this part of east London was, for 200 years or so, a very significant industrial hub, busily engaged in the manufacture and maintenance of buoys, lightships and docking equipment. It is also where, in 1911, HMS *Thunderer* was fitted out and launched, the last warship to be built on the Thames, and where the SS *Robin* was built. (Moored at St Katharine Dock and then West India Quay, the *Robin* is now part of the core collection of the National Historic Ships register, ranked alongside the *Cutty Sark*, HMS *Belfast* and *Discovery* as the oldest complete steam coaster in the world.)

All this required manpower, of course, so that, in addition to its once numerous and varied industrial buildings and wharves, this inner-city desert once boasted a school, chandlers and provisions stores, a mission, even a coffee house, and no fewer than five taverns, including the appropriately named Trinity Arms and the Steam Packet. Unfortunately, though, it was badly flooded in 1928, the population was forcibly rehoused and the area seems never to have recovered. Now littered with undistinguished and largely disused light-industrial units, it awaits the next stage in its long, slow evolution. One can only hope some small corner survives.

WOOLWICH FREE FERRY
PIER ROAD, E14

700-year-old Survivor

Woolwich being split by the river, with a small portion of it on the opposite bank in what had once been a part of Essex, one is not surprised to find that there has been a ferry here for many centuries.

There is, for example, a reference to one in state papers of 1308, when a waterman called William de Wicton sold it for £10 to William Atte, a mason. But, in fact, it probably dates back even further, to when the nearby Abbey of Lessness or Lesnes (see p. 168) was granted several parishes and manors in Essex, by Henry II and Edward I.

In time, of course, Woolwich rose to prominence as a royal dockyard and arsenal in the reigns of Henry VIII and Elizabeth I, and as London itself grew and became more crowded, the military took the decision to establish its own ferry nearby in 1810. It was not until 1880, however, that the idea took hold to fund one for the locals, and not until 23 March 1889 that the first Free Ferry steamers – *Gordon* and *Duncan* – finally replaced an old 'horse-raft' and started plying the Thames.

Incredibly, and at a cost of 8 tons of coke per vessel per day, the ferry continued using paddle-steamers right up until 1963. At that time, however, with larger trucks crowding the streets of Woolwich, and more of them too, a decision was taken to commission three new diesel-powered boats. Initially these were to operate from the old piers and then from 1966 from a new terminal a little further from the centre of town.

It was to be a sad day for their predecessors, however. After covering a total of four million miles and carrying an estimated 180 million passengers, all three were sold for scrap to Messrs Jacques Bakker and Zonen in Belgium.

None, it seems, had actually travelled as 'little ships' to Dunkirk (contrary to local legend) but they had had an honourable war nevertheless and certainly deserved a better fate than this. Plying back and forth in all weathers and in the blackout, escaping serious damage from a V1 that exploded nearby, in September 1940 they had also helped to evacuate the people of Silvertown across the burning, oily river.

But, of course, as side-loading steamers they had been conceived in an age when horse-drawn freight was the norm and traffic numbers far lower than today. Eventually the time came when they had to go; when it did they were replaced by modern end-loading vessels with a capacity of 500 passengers and 200 vehicle-tons, and new causeways to make loading and off loading easier and more efficient.

The ferry's long history has not been entirely forgotten, however, and the three boats currently in service are all named after politicians connected in some way with Woolwich and the Thames. *John Burns* (1858–1943), an astute observer of London and its river, was the first to refer to the river as 'liquid history'. *Ernest Bevin* (1881–1951) earned the nickname of 'the dockers' KC' after successfully pleading their case before a wages tribunal. And *James Newman* was mayor of Woolwich from 1923 to 1925.

ABBEY MILLS PUMPING STATION
ABBEY LANE, E15

More Cathedral than Abbey

While the Victorians are frequently associated with large-scale engineering projects as remarkable for their elaborate design and decoration as for their functional ingenuity, it takes a visit to this dismal corner of east London – and to the business end of Sir Joseph Bazalgette's mammoth main drainage scheme for London – to remind one just how far these chaps were prepared to go to perfect the purely aesthetic aspect of their great works.

Sufficiently far, that is, that with its Slavic domes and positively Byzantine interior the cheerful exuberance of the Northern Outfall Sewer's Abbey Mills Pumping Station is exceptional even without the original Moorish minarets. These were actually chimneys but, rendered redundant by the march of technology, both were eventually pulled down in the 1940s to prevent them presenting a useful marker to approaching bombers.

Locally the building is known as the cathedral to sewage, appropriately enough as when viewed from above it forms the shape of a cross. Its real name, however, derives from its proximity to a real abbey, the Cistercian Stratford Langthorne

foundation, and its adjacent twelfth-century tidal mill. Founded in 1135 by William de Montfitchet, this was one of the wealthiest Cistercian houses in the country, and, until its dissolution in 1538, was a major landowner in Newham and across much of Essex. Sadly, all that now remains of it is a single stone window in the south porch of All Saints', West Ham.

Sir Joseph's Pumping Station has clearly fared rather better, in large part because of the efforts and ingenuity of its creator who (despite building it on some very unpromising marshland) seems from the start to have been determined to leave something of lasting value.

His creation is best viewed from the Greenway, a footpath built along the top of his main sewer embankment: Sir Joseph was fortunate in having the budget to do this. In fact, the works carried out between 1860 and 1865 cost a hefty £164,000, and included machinery capable of moving an incredible 15,000 cubic feet of sewage *a minute* and the construction of no fewer than 1,300 miles of new, brick-lined sewers.

As is well known, a majority of these are still in use today, Sir Joseph having not simply sought to overcome many serious logistical challenges – the completion of the Northern Outfall, for example, required an entire railway line to be lowered and five roads to be raised – but also seeing to it that his work would prove extremely durable.

This he did by introducing a number of important quality-boosting innovations, such as the special bricks called Staffordshire Blues. Created for the lower sections of each sewer, these were specially formulated to withstand the effects of a constant flow of sewage over them. At the same time a new bonding material was employed to hold the bricks together, Bazalgette himself taking great pains to ensure that his deliveries of this newfangled Portland cement were of sufficiently good quality that the underwater joins would actually harden over time – which in the main they have.

ROYAL GUNPOWDER MILLS
BEAULIEU DRIVE, EN9

London's Other Big Bang

The strangest stretch of parkland that we see today – 170 or so tranquil acres of lawns, trees and water – was for more than 300 years the lynchpin of this country's ordnance industry. A highly secretive and enclosed world until as recently as 2001, it was here that the boffins and brass hats came to combine charcoal, sulphur and saltpetre, and later guncotton, cordite and nitro-glycerine, to provide the muscle to support Britain's imperial expansion.

Gunpowder production started here early and was already well established by 1684, the powder at that time being produced in an old mill that had previously been used for making vegetable oil. Initially privately owned and run (like its rivals at Dartford, Faversham and Hounslow) this particular facility was eventually taken over by the government in 1787 amid concerns that quality control was slipping.

It soon became pre-eminent in its field, assisted to a great degree by the diligence, discipline and expertise of Lieutenant General Sir William Congreve, Comptroller of the Royal Laboratory in Woolwich (see p. 185) and later of his son, the celebrated rocketeer and another Lieutenant General

Sir William Congreve. Indeed, by the time of the younger man's death in 1828, the Royal Gunpowder Mills were widely recognised for their scientific rigour, advanced industrial processes and highly efficient methods of manufacture.

The site grew rapidly as a result and today scores of historic buildings survive on this vast site, together with an extraordinary internal canal network (some 10 miles of water, complete with locks), although the mills' private railway system has unfortunately been dismantled.

Some periods in history were necessarily busier than others. In particular, the Napoleonic and Crimean Wars caused a huge increase in the workload, and by the First World War the mills were employing as many as 5,000 munitions works, many of them female – in 1913, the workforce had been barely a fifth of this number.

By the 1930s, however, it was becoming clear that its proximity to the capital rendered the site dangerously vulnerable to air raids. Some limited production of cordite and other important explosive materials continued here until early 1944, but the bulk of production was moved further west, beyond the range of German bombers.

Thus, by the end of the war, the factories and workshops were mostly redundant and closed up. However, still effectively in military hands, the site itself continued to function as an important research establishment until government reorganisation in 1991. Concerned not just with perfecting bigger and better bangs (explosives, of course, having important civilian uses as well as military ones) this research had encompassed rocket-propulsion systems, and the testing and evaluation of a range of advanced, high-strength materials for more specialised military and civilian applications.

Finally, in 2001, after a decade of decay and dereliction, the site was opened to the general public for the first time. Now brilliantly reinvented as part of Britain's post-industrial heritage, the historic buildings, including several unique water-, steam- and hydraulic-powered mills and press-houses, are all being gradually restored.

ACROSS LONDON

BLUE PLAQUES

Avro to Zola

Eagerly sought by homeowners keen to lend some distinction to their addresses, lobbied for by groups wishing to see distinguished lives properly recognised, and with the concept itself now much copied by other town and city authorities around the world, for nearly 150 years London's famous chocolate-brown, then blue, plaques have provided a usefully concise source of information for tourists and locals alike.

Marking places associated with writers, artists and musicians, as well as with politicians and rulers, administrators and social reformers, it is true that some individuals are now merely 'worthy' rather than highly regarded by the general public. True too, that the names of many erstwhile political giants are unlikely to be recognised even by what the official guidelines describe as 'the well-informed passer-by'. But among the more than 600 plaques – originally put in place by the Royal Society for the Arts, then the London County Council and the GLC, and now English Heritage – there are some genuine surprises, if one knows where to look for them.

At Hackford Road, for example, a plaque commemorates Vincent Van Gogh, somebody rarely if ever associated with south London but who lived in Kennington Oval in the 1870s while working for an art dealer in Southampton Row. (He later moved on to teaching and preaching at a boys' boarding school in Twickenham.) Across town, Mahatma Gandhi was resident in Baron's Court Road – taking lodgings there while studying the law – with Pakistan's founding father Mohammed Ali Jinnah living over the way in Russell Road. And Mozart wrote his first symphony not in Salzburg or Vienna, but while living on Ebury Street, SW1.

Elsewhere one finds Emile Zola exiled to the suburbs – Church Road, Upper Norwood – after the Dreyfus Affair; Napoleon III living in King Street, St James's; even Jimi Hendrix next door to Handel in Brook Street, Mayfair, who reportedly went out and bought a copy of the *Messiah* after learning of his illustrious neighbour.

Some of the very strangest, however, refer to things rather than people. Thus, the first flying bomb to fall on London is marked on a railway bridge in Bow (in Grove Road; it's actually a new plaque as the original was stolen). The first ever all-British powered flight was made by A.V. Roe on Walthamstow Marshes in 1909, his Avro No. 1 Triplane having been assembled in the arches under the nearby railway viaduct. (Strangely Short Brothers are not similarly honoured, despite commencing balloon production in a railway arch in Battersea before switching to aircraft.) And the machine gun, which like the aeroplane quickly and effectively rewrote just about every rule of warfare, was invented by American Hiram Maxim not over in the US but in his workshop at 57d Hatton Garden.

BRIDGE HOUSE ESTATES

Medieval Rents Keep the Capital on the Move

Coming by bus, cab or car, few crossing the Thames ever pause to wonder who pays for the bridges, yet for more than 700 years both the building costs and maintenance for four of the most famous ones have been met not by taxation or rates but from rents on properties accrued for precisely this purpose.

Work on the first of the quartet, a new London Bridge intended to replace a rickety wood structure, started in 1176, the builder being one Peter de Colechurch, a priest and head of the Fraternity of the Brethren of London Bridge. The religious connection sounds strange now, but was not entirely surprising then, since the Church had long encouraged the building of bridges. For centuries, as a consequence, many pious citizens of London made gifts and bequests of money or land 'to God and the Bridge' – the last such being made in 1675.

That first bridge, with its shops, houses and nineteen stone arches, took thirty-three years to complete but lasted for nearly 600. Before long it was generating not just greater cross-river trade than before, but also increased tolls, fines and rents. These, together with numerous bequests, quickly accumulated into a significant fund which, from 1243 onwards, was administered from a building on the south bank called Bridge House.

This process continued and, with growing assets in the City and surrounding countryside – in particular in the area around Borough High Street and along the riverbank here at Hay's Wharf – the so-called Bridge House Estate was able to fund the construction of a new Blackfriars Bridge in 1869, and of Tower Bridge a dozen years later; the monies were also used to purchase Southwark Bridge. Then in February 2002, the Trust assumed control of a fifth bridge when it took over the ownership and maintenance of the pedestrian-only Millennium Bridge running between Bankside and St Paul's.

In theory, this means that if one of the five collapses its reconstruction will have to be met entirely from the same fund, and to this end money is put aside each year. It seems to work too, for the fund has already been responsible for several replacement bridges, including two new London Bridges (1831 and 1972) and two Southwark ones as well, in 1819 and 1921.

Even so, many centuries of rising rents and valuable compound interest have left the Trust with more than sufficient funds for the purpose, and for some years consideration has been given to what should be done with the surplus.

With an estimated £500 million in the pot, and at least £35 million being added to it each year, one option under discussion is the construction of a new bridge to the east to take some of the traffic from Tower Bridge. In the meantime, however, the Trust has started making non-bridge-related grants to good causes thought likely to benefit Londoners. The first such grant was made in September 1995, and by 2006 the total had reached more than £170 million.

THE CROWN ESTATE

Ancient Possession, Continuing Controversy

With an estimated 12 million square feet of office space, more than 1,000 acres even excluding the Royal Parks, and literally scores of historic and world-famous buildings, Her Majesty is still by far the largest private landowner in London.

It was ever thus: historically the Church and the Crown have always held more land in the capital than any other individuals or institutions. But whereas the Church has either lost or sold much of its territory over the centuries, the Crown has managed to acquire even more of it, much of it seized from the Church during the Reformation. In fact, the Crown has disposed of very little indeed, although there is one famous exception to this: the only freehold in Pall Mall, No. 79, which was given to Nell Gwyn by Charles II after she exhorted him to 'let not poor Nelly starve'.

Today, as a consequence of many centuries of acquisition and sequestration, the estate runs from Primrose Hill to Millbank, as well as over much of Holborn, Cornhill and Smithfield in the City. Much of this is officially described as 'ancient possession', meaning it has been held by the Crown for centuries, and indeed some records proving this go back nearly a thousand years.

Other stretches have been acquired more recently, however. The land on which Regent Street is built, for example, was purchased for this purpose in the nineteenth century, and indeed the Crown Estate has continued to grow massively with the acquisition of more than 175,000 acres outside London in the last 100 years alone.

That said, it continues to be argued that none of it is any longer the personal possession of the monarch. This is because the hereditary revenues from the estate were surrendered by George III in 1760 in return for payments made in the form of the Civil List. If only it was that simple. In fact, the King's surrender was only ever deemed to be voluntary, and as each such 'voluntary surrender' lasts only for the duration of a given reign it is merely assumed (or should that be hoped?) that at the end of that reign the succeeding monarch will agree to be bound by a similarly voluntary agreement.

In other words, specifically those of the Crown Estate itself: 'The Crown Estate is not the property of the Government. Nor is it the Sovereign's private estate. It is part of the hereditary possessions of the Sovereign in right of the crown.' Or as Kevin Cahill preferred to put it in his magisterial *Who Owns Britain*: 'The Queen as Mrs Windsor does not own the Crown Estate, but Mrs Windsor as the Queen does.'

DUCHY OF CORNWALL

Kennington's Crowning Glory

While controversy might still surround the issue of who legally owns the Crown Estate, there is no such question mark over the Duchy of Cornwall. In existence since Saxon times, says historian A.L. Rowse, it belongs to the Prince of Wales, has done so for centuries and will remain the private possession of Prince Charles until the day he accedes to the throne.

Based, despite the name, not just in the west country but also in the capital south of the Thames, the duchy's London properties are chiefly clustered around what was once the Black Prince's palace in Kennington. Its owner, Edward of Woodstock (1330–76), was created Duke of Cornwall at the age of 7 – England's first ever duke – and made Prince of Wales six years after that.

Reportedly a fine soldier and for many years resident in France (where he was also Prince of Aquitaine), his Kennington estate remained an occasional royal residence until Tudor times and is today commemorated in the name of Black Prince Road, SE11. James I gave the manor of Kennington to his son Henry; and before he succeeded his father Charles I lived here too, on a house built over the site of the former palace.

Consequently, today Prince Charles, as the twenty-fourth duke, finds himself with around 128,000 acres of land in nine counties, some 230 miles of foreshore, 14,000 acres of 'fundus' or river bed and 40 acres of inner London too. The latter, said to be worth more than £400 million, comprises approximately 1,500 dwellings and several surprisingly distinctive buildings.

Of these the best known is doubtless The Oval cricket ground, but in the same neighbourhood is Kennington Park, formerly a common but now part of the duchy since James I gave it to Prince Henry. There are also some attractive twentieth-century buildings such as Courtney Square, Newquay House, Woodstock Court, and the Duchy's Old Tenants' Hostel, with its Tuscan pillared cloister and peaceful internal courtyard.

Courtney Square was built in about 1914, as part of a model estate following the slum clearances which had been effected before the First World War. With its modest Regency-style houses and pretty timber trellising, it is one of the most picturesque developments in the borough. Traditional in style, small in scale but perfectly proportioned, it provides not just attractive housing but also a very persuasive lesson in how to rebuild small, urban communities.

As such, of course, it fits in perfectly with the philosophies of the present Prince of Wales and his popular, well-argued support for the sort of architecture designed to give charm and character to a city. What he calls 'civilised architecture employing the simplest of means ... Not of the finest materials, nor richly decorated, nor on a grand scale, Courtney Square [he says] works because of its proportions and straightforward detailing.'

DUCHY OF LANCASTER

The Queen as Duke

Smaller than the Cornwall estate, but equally historic and arguably even stranger in its little idiosyncrasies, this second royal duchy comprises barely 3 acres of central London but has another 170,000 rural ones, mostly in the north. The most significant three, however, are centred on the site of the Duke of Lancaster's old Savoy Palace on the Strand; a palace, that is, which disappeared more than 500 years ago.

Its origins go back even further, though, to 1265, when Henry III, having won the Barons' War, gave his son Edmund Plantagenet land he had confiscated from two of the leading protagonists. Made Earl of Lancaster two years later and receiving the manor of the Savoy from his mother, Edmund's heirs (who included John of Gaunt) were later raised to ducal status by Edward III. In 1351 Edward also declared their territories a palatinate, thereby giving the incumbent full rights of a sovereign on his or her own land.

Most significantly, this move to create a palatine county also made the estate private rather than Crown or royal land – despite the fact that the owners were and still are clearly royal. More than six and a half centuries later this unique and (in the case of the London acres) extremely valuable status still endures.

For a while, of course, it was briefly wrested from royal hands. The duchy not long ago declared that the land belongs 'to the Sovereign of the day and has done so for some six hundred years', but in fact it was confiscated under Cromwell and in 1648 actually put up for sale by Parliament. Unsurprisingly it also changed hands several times during the Wars of the Roses, the Plantagenets' uniquely destructive family squabble. It is known too that some duchy lands were sold off by the Stuart kings, such disposals continuing until Parliament passed an Act in 1702 to prevent Queen Anne ridding herself of even more.

Today, however, the London portion holds firm, and the Queen still receives the rents from an estate encompassing Charing Cross station and the Charing Cross Hotel, Thomas Collcutt's Savoy Hotel and the adjacent theatre, and the robust little Queen's Chapel of the Savoy.

Dating back to 1510, in 1890 this last named became the first place of worship in England to be lit by electricity. Curiously, its special status, as a personal possession of the monarch rather than of a specific diocese, has also led at least one vicar to believe he could safely use it for marriages which would otherwise be illegal. From 1754 to 1756 John Wilkinson advertised his services, claiming there were 'five private ways to the Chapel, including two by water', before being caught, tried and transported. And more recently, from 1909 to 1933, another one, H.B. Chapman, sometime officer of the Divorce Reform Union, allowed both guilty and innocent parties in divorce actions to remarry here should they so wish. No such irregularities are these days permitted, although the choir still sings a unique version of the National Anthem: 'God Save our Gracious Queen, Long live our Noble Duke, God Save the Queen'.

BIBLIOGRAPHY

Unless otherwise stated all books are published in London.

Abrams, Harry N. *London*, John Russell, 1994
Arthur, Max. *Symbol of Courage*, Sidgwick & Jackson, 2004
Aslet, Clive. *The Story of Greenwich*, Fourth Estate, 1999
—— *Landmarks of Britain*, Hodder & Stoughton, 2005
Axelrod, Alan. *International Encyclopaedia of Secret Societies and Fraternal Orders*, Facts on File, 1997
Bailey, Brian. *The Guinness Book of Crime*, Guinness Publishing, 1996
Barker, Felix and Silvester-Carr, Denise. *The Black Plaque Guide to London*, Constable, 1987
Barthop, Michael. *The Armies of Britain 1485–1980*, National Army Museum, 1981
Bayley, Stephen. *Taste*, Faber, 1991
Beard, Geoffrey. *The Work of John Vanbrugh*, Universe Books, 1986
Benton, Charlotte. *A Different World. Emigré Architects in Britain 1928–1958*, RIBA, 1995
Brabbs, Derry. *England's Heritage*, Cassell & Co., 2001
Briggs, Asa. *Victorian Things*, Penguin, 1988
Brook, Stephen. *The Club: The Jews of Modern Britain*, Constable, 1989
Bryant, Sir Arthur. *Samuel Pepys: Saviour of the Navy*, William Collins, 1953
Burke, John. *Look Back on England*, Orbis, 1980
Cahill, Kevin. *Who Owns Britain*, Canongate, 2001
Cannadine, David. *The Pleasures of the Past*, Collins, 1989
—— *Aspects of Aristocracy*, Yale University Press, 1994
—— *The Decline and Fall of the British Aristocracy*, Yale University Press, 1990
Caufield, Catherine. *The Emperor of the United States of America and Other Magnificent British Eccentrics*, Routledge & Kegan Paul, 1981
Clark, Sir G. (ed.). *The Oxford History of England* (16 vols), Oxford University Press, 1975
Clifton-Taylor, Alec. *Buildings of Delight*, Gollancz, 1988
Clout, Hugh (ed.). *London History Atlas*, Times Books, 1991
Clunn, Harold P. *The Face of London*, Spring Books, 1957
Deighton, Len. *London Dossier*, Jonathan Cape, 1967

Dictionary of National Biography, Oxford University Press, 1975

Dimbleby, Jonathan. *The Prince of Wales*, Little, Brown, 1994

Donaldson, William. *Brewer's Rogues, Villains & Eccentrics*, Cassell, 2002

Duncan, Andrew. *Secret London*, New Holland, 2003

Durant, G.M. *Britain: Rome's Most Northerly Province*, G. Bell & Sons, 1969

Earl, Peter. *A City Full of People*, Methuen, 1994

English Heritage. *The Blue Plaque Guide*, Journeyman Press, 1991

—— *London's Town Halls*, English Heritage, 1999

Fairfield, Sheila. *The Streets of London*, Papermac, 1983

Falconer, Keith. *England's Industrial Heritage*, Batsford, 1980

Fara, Patricia. *Newton: The Making of Genius*, Macmillan, 2002

Fellows, Richard. *Edwardian Architecture*, Lund Humphries, 1995

Field, Lesley. *Bendor*, Weidenfeld & Nicolson, 1983

Fletcher, Sir Banister. *A History of Architecture*, (18th ed.), Athlone Press, 1975

Fletcher, Geoffrey. *The London Nobody Knows*, Penguin, 1965

Fraser, Antonia. *King Charles II*, Weidenfeld & Nicolson, 1979

Frere, Sheppard. *Britannia: A History of Roman Britain*, Routledge & Kegan Paul, 1967

Friar, Stephen. *The Companion to English Parish Churches*, Sutton Publishing, 1996

Galinou, Mireille (ed.). *London's Pride*, Anaya, 1990

Gardiner, Julia (ed.). *Who's Who in British History*, Collins & Brown, 2000

Gaunt, William. *Victorian Olympus*, Jonathan Cape, 1975

Girling, Brian. *Westminster's Villages*, Chalford Publishing, 1996

Greenwood, Douglas. *Who's Buried Where In England*, Constable, 1982

Halliday, Stephen. *Newgate: London's Prototype of Hell*, Sutton Publishing, 2006

Hanson, Neil. *The Dreadful Judgement: The True Story of the Great Fire*, Doubleday, 2001

Hibbert, Christopher. *Tower of London*, Newsweek, 1971

—— *The Court of St James's*, Weidenfeld & Nicolson, 1979

—— and Weinreb, Ben. *The London Encyclopaedia*, Macmillan, 1983

HRH The Prince of Wales. *A Vision of Britain*, Doubleday, 1989

Ironbridge Gorge Museum Trust. *The Ironbridge Gorge*, Jarrold, 1996

Jackson, Peter. *Walks in Old London*, Brockhampton Press, 1995

Jardine, Lisa. *Ingenious Pursuits*, Little, Brown, 1999

Jenkins, Simon. *City at Risk*, Hutchinson, 1970

—— *England's Thousand Best Churches*, Allen Lane, 1999

Jenner, Michael. *The Architectural History of Britain & Ireland*, Michael Joseph, 1995

Jones, Edward and Woodward, Christopher. *A Guide to the Architecture of London*, Seven Dials, 2000

Kent, William. *London for Everyman*, J.M. Dent & Sons, 1938

—— *An Encyclopaedia of London*, Dent & Sons, 1970

Kerr, Nigel (ed.). *John Betjeman's Guide to English Parish Churches*, HarperCollins, 1993

—— and Kerr, Mary. *Medieval Sites in Britain*, Diamond Books, 1988

Kightly, Charles. *The Customs and Ceremonies of Britain*, Thames & Hudson, 1986

Kingsbury, Pamela D. *Lord Burlington's Town Architecture*, RIBA, 1995

Kostof, Spiro. *The City Shaped*, Thames & Hudson, 1991

—— *The City Assembled*, Thames & Hudson, 1992

Lacey, Robert. *Aristocrats*, Hutchinson, 1983

Leapman, Michael (ed.). *The Book of London*, Weidenfeld & Nicolson, 1992

Lees-Milne, James. *Earls of Creation*, Penguin, 2001

Long, David. *Spectacular Vernacular: London's 100 Most Extraordinary Buildings*, Sutton Publishing, 2006

Lowe, Jacques and McLachlan, Sandy. *The City*, Quartet/Visual Arts, 1982

Lycett Green, Candida. *England: Travels Through An Unwrecked Landscape*, Pavilion, 1996

Mace, Rodney. *Trafalgar Square: Emblem of Empire*, Lawrence & Wishart, 2005

Masters, Brian. *The Dukes*, Pimlico, 2001

Mee, Arthur. *Surrey*, Hodder & Stoughton, 1938

Merullo, Annabel (ed.). *British Greats*, Cassell, 2000

Michell, John. *Sacred England*, Gothic Image Publications, 2003

Milne, Gustav. *Roman London*, English Heritage/B.T. Batsford, 1995

Moore, Tim. *Do Not Pass Go*, Vintage, 2003

Mordaunt Crook, J. *The Greek Revival*, RIBA/Country Life, 1968

Norwich, John Julius (ed.). *The Duff Cooper Diaries*, Weidenfeld & Nicolson, 2005

Ormsby Gore, Rt. Hon. W. *Ancient Monuments, Vol. II. Southern England*, HMSO, 1936

Paxman, Jeremy. *The English*, Michael Joseph, 1998

Pearce, David. *The Great Houses of London*, Vendome Press, 1986

Pevsner, Nikolaus. *Buildings of England: London* (2 vols), Penguin, 1952, 1962

Picard, Lisa. *Restoration London*, Weidenfeld & Nicolson, 1997

—— *Dr Johnson's London*, Weidenfeld & Nicolson, 2000

—— *Elizabeth's London*, Weidenfeld & Nicolson, 2003

—— *Victorian London*, Weidenfeld & Nicolson, 2005

Piper, David. *The Companion Guide to London*, Collins, 1964

Plimmer, Charlotte and Denis. *London*, Batsford, 1977

Plumb, J.H. and Wheldon, Huw. *Royal Heritage*, BBC, 1977

Pollins, Harold. *Economic History of the Jews in England*, Associated University Presses, 1982

Pottle, F.A. (ed.). *Boswell's London Journal 1762–1763*, Heinemann, 1950

Rodger, N.A.M. *The Command of the Ocean: A Naval History of Britain, Vol. II 1649–1815*, Allen Lane, 2004

Rowlandson, T. and Pugin, A.C. *The Microcosm of London*, King Penguin, 1947

Saint, Andrew and Darley, Gillian. *The Chronicles of London*, Weidenfeld & Nicolson, 1994

Saunders, Ann. *The Art and Architecture of London*, Phaidon, 1988

Scruton, Roger. 'Hail Quinlan Terry', *Spectator*, 8 April 2006

Seymour, R. *Survey of the Cities of London and Westminster*, 1735

Simon, Kate. *London. Places and Pleasures*, MacGibbon & Kee, 1968

Sinclair, Iain and Atkins, Marc. *Liquid City*, Reaktion, 1999

Stow, John. *The Survey of London*, 1598

Strong, Roy. *The Renaissance Garden in England*, Thames & Hudson, 1979

—— *Lost Treasures of Britain*, Viking, 1990

Summerson, John. *Georgian London*, Yale University Press, 2003

Sykes, Christopher Simon. *Private Palaces*, Chatto & Windus, 1985

Thornton, Peter. *A New Description of Sir John Soane's Museum*, published by the Trustees, 1966

Trench, Richard and Hillman, Ellis. *London Under London*, John Murray, 1984

Trevelyan, G. M. *History of England*, Longmans, Green & Co., 1943

Vogt, A.M. *The Nineteenth Century*, Herbert Press, 1989

Walford, Edward. *Greater London*, Cassell & Co., 1884

Weinreb, Matthew. *London Architecture Features and Façades*, Phaidon, 1993

White, Colin. *The Trafalgar Captains*, Chatham Publishing, 2005

Ziegler, Philip. *The Black Death*, Collins, 1969